Roberta Bondar

CANADA'S FIRST WOMAN IN SPACE

By Judy Wearing

Crabtree Publishing Company
www.crabtreebooks.com

Crabtree Publishing Company

www.crabtreebooks.com

Author: Judy Wearing
Publishing plan research and development:
  Sean Charlebois, Reagan Miller
  Crabtree Publishing Company
Editors: Mark Sachner, Lynn Peppas
Proofreader: Wendy Scavuzzo
Indexer: Wendy Scavuzzo
Editorial director: Kathy Middleton
Photo researcher: Ruth Owen
Designer: Alix Wood
Production coordinator: Margaret Amy Salter
Production: Kim Richardson
Prepress technician: Margaret Amy Salter

Written, developed, and produced by
Water Buffalo Books

Publisher's note:
All quotations in this book come from original sources and contain the spelling and grammatical inconsistencies of the original text. The use of such constructions is for the sake of preserving the historical and literary accuracy of the sources.

Photographs and reproductions:
Roberta Bondar: page 93; page 97; page 103
Canadian Space Agency: page 31 (all); page 50
Flickr (Creative Commons): page 102
IMAX/Destiny in Space: page 69
NASA Images: front cover (all); page 1; page 4 (inset);
    page 5; page 7; page 9; page 11; page 15; page 17;
    page 19; page 22; page 29; page 37 (all); page 39;
    page 41; page 43; page 45; page 47; page 49; page 51;
    page 53; page 55; page 57; page 61; page 64; page 67;
    page 77; page 79; page 81; page 83; page 86; page 95;
    page 101
Shutterstock: page 4 (background); page 13;
    page 24; page 33; page 42; page 56; page 59; page 62;
    page 73; page 76; page 90
Wikipedia (public domain): page 21; page 23

Cover: In 1992 scientist Roberta Bondar became Canada's first female astronaut when she boarded the space shuttle *Discovery*. She and crewmate Steve Oswald are shown here working in the IML (International Microgravity Laboratory) as part of the mission's study of the effects of low gravity on humans.

Library and Archives Canada Cataloguing in Publication

Wearing, Judy
    Roberta Bondar : Canada's first woman in space /
Judy Wearing.

(Crabtree groundbreaker biographies)
Includes index.
Issued also in an electronic format.
ISBN 978-0-7787-2540-4 (bound).--ISBN 978-0-7787-2549-7 (pbk.)

    1. Bondar, Roberta Lynn, 1945- --Juvenile literature.
2. Women astronauts--Canada--Biography--Juvenile literature.
3. Astronauts--Canada--Biography--Juvenile literature.
4. Environmentalists--Canada--Biography--Juvenile literature.
5. Environmental protection--Juvenile literature. 6. Nature
conservation--Juvenile literature. I. Title. II. Series: Crabtree
groundbreaker biographies

TL789.85.B66W42 2011   j629.450092   C2010-903028-1

Library of Congress Cataloging-in-Publication Data

Wearing, Judy.
  Roberta Bondar : Canada's first woman in space /
Judy Wearing.
       p. cm. -- (Crabtree groundbreaker biographies)
  Includes index.
  ISBN 978-0-7787-2549-7 (pbk. : alk. paper) --
ISBN 978-0-7787-2540-4 (reinforced library binding : alk.
paper) -- ISBN 978-1-4271-9472-5 (electronic (PDF))
  1. Bondar, Roberta, 1945---Juvenile literature. 2. Women
astronauts--Canada--Biography--Juvenile literature. 3.
Astronauts--Canada--Biography--Juvenile literature. 4.
Environmentalists--Canada--Biography--Juvenile literature.
5. Environmental protection--Juvenile literature. 6. Nature
conservation--Juvenile literature. I. Title. II. Series.

  TL789.85.B66W43 2011
  629.450092--dc22
  [B]
                                    2010018046

Crabtree Publishing Company

www.crabtreebooks.com   1-800-387-7650

Printed in the USA/082010/BL20100723

**Published in
Canada**
Crabtree Publishing
616 Welland Ave.
St. Catharines, Ontario
L2M 5V6

**Published in
the United States**
Crabtree Publishing
PMB 59051
350 Fifth Avenue, 59th Floor
New York, New York 10118

**Published in
the United Kingdom**
Crabtree Publishing
Maritime House
Basin Road North, Hove
BN41 1WR

**Published in
Australia**
Crabtree Publishing
386 Mt. Alexander Rd.
Ascot Vale (Melbourne)
VIC 3032

Contents

Chapter 1
A Dream Come True

Roberta Bondar opens her eyes. It is 3:00 a.m., January 22, 1992. For a second, she forgets where she is, then remembers she's in Florida, at the Kennedy Space Center. She's been living in a dormitory with six men for the last week in quarantine. She has not been allowed to go anywhere, and everyone she has seen has been carefully checked over by doctors first. Roberta hasn't minded this isolation. She knows it is important to make sure that neither she, nor any of the other six, is carrying an infection that could make them sick. They've been busy working, so the time has gone quickly.

She is calm; she is ready. She's been training for over a year. She's also excited—this is a moment she's been waiting for since she was a little girl.

Opposite: Roberta Bondar was so moved by her view of Earth as seen from space that she dedicated herself to helping the planet, following her retirement as an astronaut.

Morning Preparations

Roberta eats breakfast with the rest of the space shuttle crew. She is calm; she is ready. She's been training for over a year. She's also excited—this is a moment she's been waiting for since she was a little girl. Everyone is excited! At 6:30 a.m., the crew members enter the "clean room." There are seven body suits here, one for each of them. The suits are exactly the same color as the paint on the Golden Gate Bridge in San Francisco—International Orange. The bright orange makes the crew easy to see, in case they have to exit the shuttle in an emergency and end up in the ocean, waiting to be rescued. The suit has a black ring around the neck—where a helmet will be attached later. Everyone is wearing the same gray socks, the same pale blue underwear, and the same black boots—in their own size, of course. It takes about 20 minutes to get dressed into their launch/entry suits, which they call LES for short. Roberta knows that her LES will protect her from the heat and air pressure changes her body is going to endure on the trip into space. She's glad she's got it, even if it does weigh a total of 90 pounds (41 kg). Roberta feels the weight, but she is used to it. They've been wearing a similar suit during training.

Roberta looks down briefly at the patch on her suit, on the right side of her chest. It is a picture of the shiny silver shuttle up in space. She and her crewmates designed the patch themselves. Each mission has a different patch. Her name, *BONDAR*, is in capital letters on the outside of the patch with a little red Canadian

The official STS–42 crew portrait, from left to right: Stephen S. Oswald, pilot; Roberta L. Bondar, payload specialist 1; Norman E. Thagard, mission specialist 1; Ronald J. Grabe, commander; David C. Hilmers, mission specialist 2; Ulf D. Merbold, payload specialist 2; and William F. Readdy, mission specialist 3. Mission STS–42 was launched aboard the space shuttle Discovery *on January 22, 1992 at 9:52:33 a.m. (Eastern Standard Time).*

maple leaf beside it. There are six other names on the patch, those of the other crew members: *HILMERS, THAGARD, MERBOLD, OSWALD, GRABE,* and *READDY.* Each of them has prepared for years for this journey. Each of them has friends and family hoping that they will return safe and sound. Two of them have been on a shuttle three times before, one of them twice before, another once before. Roberta and two others have never been in space. This space shuttle is called *Discovery.*

The seven crew members walk outside their quarters to a white van waiting to take them to the launch pad. It is still dark outside, but it is calm and there is not a cloud in the sky—a perfect day for a shuttle launch. A few reporters and television cameras are there to watch the departure.

Roberta waves excitedly. A voice calls, "Roberta! Roberta!" It is the Canadian media—and when Roberta sees them she puts both hands up in the air and grins from ear to ear, yelling, "Yes! Yes!" The reporter asks her, "How are you feeling?" Roberta replies, "Well rested," and hops into the van.

Countdown to Liftoff

At the launch pad, the crew members take their last steps on land before entering the elevator that takes them up 195 feet (60 m) to a room just outside the shuttle entrance. Several NASA staff members help them finish dressing. Roberta is assisted into her parachute harness, communications hat, helmet, and gloves. She and her colleagues are all escorted to their seats in the shuttle, located in the crew module

THE KENNEDY SPACE CENTER

President Dwight D. Eisenhower created NASA—the National Aeronautics and Space Administration—in 1958, years before anyone had been in space. Four years later, when the first attempts to land spacecraft on the Moon began, 219 square miles (567 sq km) on the east coast of Florida was selected as the site of the launch into space. This launch site was named the Kennedy Space Center in 1963, in honor of slain U.S. president, John F. Kennedy. The Kennedy Space Center is still the location of all NASA space launches.

The STS–42 Mission insignia includes clusters of four and two stars that represent Mission STS–42; an isolated star in memory of former crew member Sonny Carter, who died in a commercial plane crash; and "IML-1," which stands for "International Microgravity Laboratory-1," which is the name of the laboratory the shuttle is bringing to space to carry out experiments on the effects of low gravity.

at the front of the orbiter—the main part of the shuttle that has wings, like a plane. In the cockpit, also called the flight deck, where the pilot and commander sit, there is room for four people. So Roberta and two others are on a floor below the cockpit, in the middle of the crew module, called the mid-deck. Their three chairs will be folded up and put away once the shuttle is in space.

Roberta is strapped into her chair, flat on her back. Her knees are bent, and her thighs point straight up. It will be several hours before she will be able to move, once the shuttle has reached its destination in space. She is wearing a kind of diaper, as are all the astronauts, so that they can empty their bladders when they need to, while strapped into their chairs.

While waiting, the crew has a long checklist to go through to make sure all of their equipment is ready. People on the ground have been working all night to fill the large, brown-colored tank with liquid fuel. They've been checking and rechecking all the instruments to make sure everything is working properly. A group of family and friends waits for take-off about three miles (five km) away from the launch pad. Roberta feels impatient. She can't look out the mid-deck's window. It is covered with a metal shield. The room is in semidarkness, with only an eerie green glow from special chemical lights—like the glow sticks children

"... I feel like a goldfish with an anchor...."

Roberta Bondar, writing in her memoir *Touching the Earth*

The space shuttle Discovery *hitches a ride on NASA's modified Boeing 747 Shuttle Carrier Aircraft. The chart below offers some statistics that show ways in which the space shuttle measures up against a Boeing 747.*

Feature	Boeing 747–400	*Discovery*
Length	231 ft (70 m)	122 ft (37 m)
Wingspan	211 ft (64 m)	78 ft (24 m)
Weight	399,000 lbs (181,000 kg)	230,000 lbs (104,326 kg)
Maximum cargo	249,122 lbs (113,000 kg)	63,500 lbs (28,803 kg)
Speed	583 mph (938 KPH)	17,321 mph (27,875 KPH)

sometimes wear around their necks. She can't move her head very well because of her helmet.

Close to launch, the astronauts and ground control are running through the instruments. Ground control is listing the fuel cells, which provide power for the shuttle up in space, and the crew is reporting whether the indicators say they are working or not. "LRD," hears Roberta through her communication helmet. "LRD is go," replies her crewmate. "FRO," says ground control. "FRO is no go" is the response. There seems to be a problem.

Roberta doesn't move. She stays strapped in her chair and waits. The engineers work on sorting things out. In about an hour, the issue is corrected, and the shuttle is going to launch as planned. "Have a good flight and a safe landing," she hears. Then, "Three. Two. One. Zero. And liftoff!"

The Trip into Space

At 9:53 a.m., Roberta feels the shuttle shift around her. The three orbiter engines have started. The orbiter engines do not have enough power on their own to lift *Discovery*, its rockets, and its fuel tank off the ground. A few seconds later, the solid rocket boosters attached to the big fuel tank are fired. There is a loud rumbling noise, and Roberta is aware that she is moving. For the next two minutes and six seconds, Roberta and the rest of the crew shake, their seats shake, and the shuttle shakes as the whole structure is pushed away from Earth's surface by the power of the attached rocket boosters. Once the rockets are firing, there is no way to stop them. This part of liftoff is

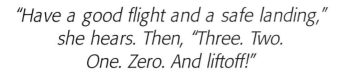

"Have a good flight and a safe landing,"
she hears. Then, "Three. Two.
One. Zero. And liftoff!"

particularly nerve-racking.

Then, the shaking subsides, and Roberta knows the solid rocket boosters have separated from the shuttle. The ride out of Earth's atmosphere and into space is not over yet, however. The shuttle is now about 30 miles (48 km) from Earth. The engines of the orbiter use the fuel from the external fuel tank to continue the journey.

At seven minutes after liftoff, Roberta feels as though her whole body is being crushed. The shuttle has to go extremely fast to achieve its orbit around Earth. The shuttle increases speed so quickly that she has three times the force of gravity pushing against her.

At about eight minutes since it left the launch pad, the shuttle's fuel is consumed, the fuel tank separates and falls away, and the main engines stop. They are 184 miles (296 km) up from home, moving at a speed of nearly 17,500 miles per hour (28,163 KPH). There is nothing in space to slow them down, so the shuttle—and everything in it— will continue to move at that speed for the entire time they are there. They will circle Earth over and over; they are in orbit. Earth's gravity will pull on them a little bit, and the shuttle will fall one-half mile (one km) every day, but the astronauts no longer feel any force against them. That only happens when they accelerate.

The shuttle's pilot steers the shuttle into the correct position—with its tail pointing toward Earth. This position minimizes the pull of gravity on the shuttle. All is still. Roberta will soon unbuckle her straps and float out of her chair. She is the first neurologist and the first Canadian woman in space.

Discovery is officially in orbit, and Roberta has a lot of work to do. She is in charge of all the biology and medical experiments on the mission. First, however, she will have a childhood dream come true; she will make her way to the flight deck and look out the windows at the turquoise blue planet that we call home.

> "I push off the flight-deck floor and head towards the windows in the aft flight deck. The lump in my throat gives way to a murmur then a stifled cry. There it is. All the View-Master reels and all the shuttle photographs did not prepare me for this emotional rendezvous with the planet that I had lived upon, studied, and thought I knew."
>
> Roberta Bondar in
> *Touching the Earth*

The launch of space shuttle Discovery on January 22, 1992, at 9:52 a.m. EST, from Kennedy Space Center, Florida, with Roberta Bondar onboard. Over the course of the mission, which lasted until January 30, Roberta performed a number of experiments in the shuttle's reusable International Microgravity Laboratory, or IML.

Chapter 2
An Astronaut in the Making

Roberta Bondar was born on December 2, 1945, in Sault Ste. Marie, Ontario, Canada. Her father, Edward, was an office manager who worked for the city. Her mother, Mildred, was a teacher who taught business. Roberta has one sister, Barbara, who is a year older. By the time she was eight years old, Roberta was utterly obsessed with space. She spent much of every day pretending to be in space or on her way to space.

A Head for Space

While Roberta's body—and most of her mind—was on Earth, she led an active imaginary life in which she spoke with beings from outer space on her radio set. She and her sister read

As a girl, Roberta had a space station in her bedroom, along with a plywood spaceship with cockpit controls made of wire.

science fiction books and comics featuring space adventurers like Flash Gordon and Buck Rogers. These characters traveled through the galaxies fighting bad guys, decades before James T. Kirk from *Star Trek* and Han Solo from *Star Wars* were created.

Roberta and Barbara got many ideas from these books for their pretend space missions. The girls also listened to science fiction programs on the radio and watched every science fiction movie they could on television. Science fiction movies such as *It Came from Outer Space* were very popular at the time, though the endings were sometimes too scary for Roberta, so her mom had to watch them for her and tell her what happened afterward.

As a girl, Roberta had a space station in her bedroom, along with a plywood spaceship with cockpit controls made of wire. One time, she and Barbara sent away for "space helmets" from the Dubble Bubble chewing gum company. They were disappointed when the packages arrived in flat, brown envelopes. Roberta had hoped for a real-looking helmet with a glass cover and an air hose. Instead, what she got was made from white cardboard which, when unfolded, formed a tall and square box with a large opening in the front. The box sat on her shoulders and, even though it wasn't as realistic as she had hoped, the two sisters wore their helmets anyway on their space missions in their Sault Ste. Marie neighborhood.

The girls brought along supplies for these missions, such as food and drink, and armed themselves against any nasty aliens with water pistols—bright red and green ones that looked

Roberta Bondar's official NASA portrait. When she sent away for a toy "space helmet" as a young girl, she could not have imagined the kind of helmet she would one day wear as an astronaut!

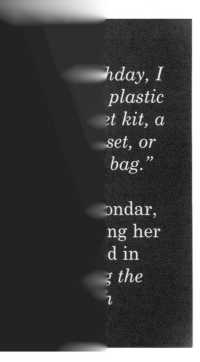

hday, I
plastic
et kit, a
set, or
bag."

ondar,
ng her
d in
g the
n

just like the ray guns Flash Gordon used.

Roberta's love of space continued throughout adolescence. While on camping trips with her family on the wild shores of Lake Superior, the sisters explored new "planets," taking note of soils and plants as well as any strange, "humanlike" life forms nearby. With her Brownie camera—a simple, inexpensive way to take black-and-white photographs—Roberta captured the worlds she explored. Her parents were very encouraging of Roberta's interests, and, in addition to taking her camping, they enrolled her in Girl Guides of Canada and the YMCA, where she developed many life skills.

When Roberta was seven, her father built a chemistry laboratory in the family basement, so she could do experiments. (The famous inventor Thomas Edison also had a basement chemistry lab as a child.) An aunt

When Roberta was seven, her father built a chemistry laboratory in the family basement, so she could do experiments.

and uncle involved with NASA during Roberta's teenage years sent her clippings and photographs, which she displayed on the walls of her bedroom.

Teenage Roberta won awards at science fairs and kept caterpillars in her bathroom for a time. She spent her summers working for the Department of Fisheries and Forestry of the Canadian government. Her job was to help with the study of an insect that does great damage to coniferous trees, including the vast stretches of boreal forest that surrounded her hometown. For six summers, Roberta worked in a laboratory studying the genetics of the spruce budworm, trying to understand how its visual system works.

Roberta never ceased to view life as an adventure.

Off to University

Roberta's summer job studying spruce budworm led her to pursue a career in biology. After high school, she moved to southern Ontario to attend the University of Guelph, where she studied

FANTASTIC SIGHTS LEAP AT YOU

IN 3-DIMENSION

AMAZING! EXCITING! SPECTACULAR!

IT CAME FROM OUTER SPACE

From Ray Bradbury's great science fiction story!

— Starring —
Richard CARLSON · Barbara RUSH
with CHARLES DRAKE · RUSSELL JOHNSON
KATHLEEN HUGHES · JOE SAWYER

Directed by JACK ARNOLD · Screenplay by HARRY ESSEX · Produced by WILLIAM ALLAND · A UNIVERSAL-INTERNATIONAL PICTURE

A 1953 movie poster for It Came from Outer Space. *Science fiction was big in the 1950s, and the variety of sci-fi books, TV, radio, and movies all fed Roberta's desire to one day travel in outer space.*

zoology and agriculture. In 1968, she graduated with her first degree—a Bachelor of Science. Her next degree was a Master of Science in pathology, from the University of Western Ontario. Pathology is the study of disease and, in her studies, Roberta found herself heading down the path toward medicine.

Roberta's third degree, from the University of Toronto, was in neurobiology. She had found her specialty—and she would continue to study the nervous system for the rest of her adult life. Then, she attended a fourth university— McMaster University in Hamilton, Ontario— and became a Doctor of Medicine. The year was 1977, and Roberta had spent a total of 13 years in university.

After four more years of training, Roberta became a full-fledged doctor with a specialty in neurology—nerve medicine. She treated people who had problems with their nervous system and did research to learn more about how our nervous system works. In her research, Roberta explored how the inner ear and its balancing system relate to the function of the eyes. Her dream of going to space seemed not to be an option. Canada had no astronaut space program, and NASA did not take Canadians on its missions. NASA was choosing its astronauts at the time from among its best U.S. jet pilots.

Astronauts Wanted

On July 14, 1983, a want ad appeared in the jobs and careers section of Canadian newspapers. The ad was placed by the National Research Council Canada, which is in charge of funding for scientific research. It invited qualified

Scott Crossfield is shown in the cockpit of the Douglas D–558–II Skyrocket, a jet- and rocket-powered plane, after becoming the first person to fly at Mach 2 (twice the speed of sound).

LONGING FOR SPACE IN 1953

While Roberta and her sister, Barbara, were pretending to be astronauts, people around the world were captivated by the idea of going into space. Space travel in the real world, however, was not yet established. The U.S. government was still testing the effects that leaving Earth had on living things.

In 1953, when Roberta was eight, the U.S. government made 26 experimental flights into space with balloons, most of which carried a capsule containing animals such as flies, mice, hamsters, cats, and dogs. Sometimes the capsules were recovered and the animals were alive; sometimes they were not recovered or, if they were found, the animals inside had died. Also in 1953, the U.S. military launched a new missile, called Redstone, which would one day become part of the launching technology that put a science satellite into orbit around Earth.

Other advances were made in human flight in 1953. A speed record was broken when pilot Scott Crossfield flew a jet- and rocket-powered plane at more than Mach 2 (twice the speed of sound) or more than 1,320 miles per hour (2,124 KPH). This was quite an achievement but was still a far cry from 25 times the speed of sound—the speed at which the *Discovery* shuttle flies!

Roberta was 16 years old when the first human flew in space. Yuri Gagarin of the former Soviet Union (now Russia and several other independent republics, such as Ukraine, Georgia, and Kazakhstan) orbited Earth on his own in a spacecraft—and came back down to tell about it—in 1961.

A newspaper reports the successful flight of the first human in space, Soviet cosmonaut Yuri Gagarin, on April 12, 1961. As the headlines on the paper indicate, there was a real sense of urgency in the United States to beat the Soviet Union during the "Space Race" of the 1950s and 1960s.

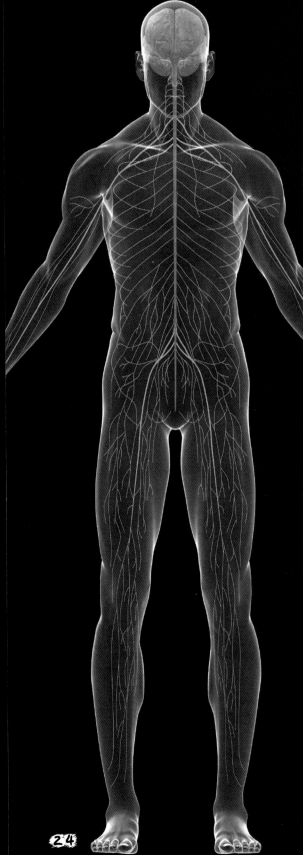

NERVE MEDICINE

Neurology is the study of medicine of the nervous system, including all nervous tissue in the body: the brain, spinal cord, and all 45 miles (72 km) or so of nerves from the top of the head to the tips of the toes. Neurologists are medical doctors who have extra training in the way the nervous system works and the problems that can occur with it.

Since nerves control all aspects of body function, many diseases and conditions have a nervous-system component. Some of the best-known medical problems that neurologists treat and research include brain and spinal injuries, cerebral palsy, meningitis, multiple sclerosis, Parkinson's disease, sleep disorders, and stroke. In the United States and Canada, it takes at least 12 years of training to become a neurologist.

Artwork showing the human nervous system, which includes the brain, the spinal cord, and a vast network of nerves that cover the entire body.

Canadian men and women to apply for a job for three years "to fly as astronauts on future space shuttle missions." The job description included helping develop two sets of experiments to be performed aboard the space shuttle, talking to the Canadian public about space flight and, if selected to be an astronaut by NASA, carrying out one of the experiments in space.

The ad also described the necessary qualifications—university degrees, experience in either engineering or physiology, and excellent health. Flying experience was valuable, as was the ability to communicate in English and French. The salary for the job was $40,000 to $55,000 a year—which was less than half the salary of a specialized medical doctor at the time. A total of six qualified people were to be hired.

This job was created because NASA had just issued a formal invitation for Canadian astronauts to take part in their space flight program as payload specialists. Canada was to choose the astronauts who could take part, but NASA had final say on whether a person would be allowed on a particular mission. One requirement for mission participation would be meeting NASA's medical standards.

Roberta heard about the astronaut job on the radio. To her, it seemed as though NASA was asking, "Roberta, where are you?" Her application was on its way to the NRC the very next day. She was not the only one who wanted the job, however. Applications came pouring in from all over Canada. The research council expected to receive about 1,000 applications. In the end, they received almost 4,400 applications from people who ranged in age from six to 73.

There were poets and journalists, firefighters and skydivers, engineers and scientists—all of them looking for a chance to go into space. The NRC was impressed by the "sincere desire expressed by all applicants to be a Canadian astronaut." The NRC wrote back personal letters to the children who responded to the ad. Roberta had a lot of competition.

In a couple of months, the list was whittled down to 1,800 candidates, all of whom had the basic credentials. The next step was to focus on their physical health. Did they have trouble sleeping? Were they prone to worry? Did they suffer from motion sickness? Doctors looked at the answers supplied to questions like these and chose 68 people to interview. Roberta was one of them. She was working as a doctor in Hamilton at the time, and her patients were delighted. The list of 68 was cut down to 19 and, again, Roberta had made the cut.

When the call reached Roberta Bondar to tell her she'd been selected as one of six Canadians to become an astronaut, she was sitting at the dinner table with her family, celebrating her thirty-eighth birthday.

> *"Now interspace craft are so small*
> *That astronauts must not be tall.*
> *They'd need bigger suits and seats*
> *And have you seen what a grown man eats?!*
> *Oh, no. The perfect candidate*
> *Must be small in height and light of weight.*
>
> *I'm barely pushing five foot three*
> *So there's no better choice than me!*
> *My boss has promised it's okay*
> *To take time off without my pay*
> *'Cause he thinks I'm already gone*
> *Far from the earth we're standing on."*
>
> Canadian astronaut applicant Deborah
> Knight-Nikifortchuk

These hopefuls were brought together in Ottawa for a full week of interviews and medical tests. They also had to give a ten-minute speech to the hiring committee of 12 to prove their communication skills.

When the call reached Roberta Bondar to tell her she'd been selected as one of six Canadians to become an astronaut, she was sitting at the dinner table with her family, celebrating her thirty-eighth birthday. What a birthday present! Within a month, she and her five colleagues had left their jobs and their homes and moved to Ottawa to start training. Soon afterward, they received the news that NASA had invited a Canadian to come on a shuttle mission in October—only ten months away.

Can a Girl Go into Space?

In 1969, Neil Armstrong became the first person to walk on the Moon. As part of the Canadian Broadcasting Corporation's news coverage, a CBC television reporter interviewed children on a playground to get their thoughts about the Moon walk accomplishment. The reporter asked a young girl, "Would you like to go on the Moon?" Without hesitating, she nodded her head and spoke clearly, "Yes."

"Do you think you will?"

"No" replied the girl with a shake of her head, again sure of her answer.

"Why not?" asked the reporter?

"Because I'm not a boy," responded the girl. She knew the way things stood—and they remained that way for many years. One woman had traveled into space—Soviet cosmonaut Valentina Tereshkova, who in 1963 spent three days orbiting Earth in a solo flight. It would be another 20 years before a woman again orbited our planet. American Sally Ride was one of six female NASA astronauts, out of a total of 35, chosen in 1978. In 1983, she was a mission specialist on Mission STS–7, aboard the space shuttle *Challenger*.

The same year, 1983, Roberta was the only woman chosen as a Canadian astronaut in the job competition. This was a big deal, as female astronauts were still quite rare, and Roberta was questioned repeatedly and constantly by

THREE KINDS OF ASTRONAUTS

The word astronaut *loosely means "space sailor" in Greek, but astronauts are not sailors. The word refers specifically to people who go up in space with NASA; the people who go up in space with the Russian (and former Soviet) space program are called* cosmonauts. *There are three kinds of* astronauts. Pilot astronauts *guide the shuttle's flight from liftoff to landing. To become a pilot astronaut, a person needs to have flown a jet at least 1,000 hours.* Mission specialists *are scientists and engineers. They do not fly the spacecraft but manage the crew activity, including food consumption and operation of all equipment, and conduct experiments. They are often engineers by training.* Payload specialists *are not NASA employees. They have specialized duties on a mission that relate to the mission's particular purpose. Payload specialists are the only kind of astronaut who can have a nationality other than American. Although their duties may differ from those of other crew members, payload specialists must still train extensively.*

the press about the fact she was a woman. Many speculated that she was chosen only because she was a woman, to make the public feel good, rather than because she was the best person for the job. This talk annoyed Roberta, who did not want to be considered as second best. She said, "no one likes to be referred to as a token about anything in life."

While Roberta understood that it was good for Canadians to have a female role model in her unusual job, she also thought it was a little sad that the fact she was a woman was of interest in the first place! "A hundred years from now, people will be shaking their heads and saying, 'what's it all about?'" The question of whether Roberta was chosen for the job because of her gender or because of her ability would haunt her.

...man, there will
...n there because
...g the best."

...er of the
...ronaut hiring
...ee, 1983

The Ups and Downs of Space Training

Part of Roberta's astronaut training was to conduct motion-sickness research. She and the other astronauts put themselves in various machines to cause motion sickness and then carefully observed the results. The astronauts were spun backwards, dropped rapidly, or rotated while blindfolded. They were also put in a chamber that mimicked the conditions of high altitude—low air pressure and low oxygen.

CANADA'S FIRST SIX ASTRONAUTS, 1983

Marc Garneau, engineer and navy officer

Roberta Bondar, doctor and neurologist

Steve MacLean, astrophysicist

Bob Thirsk, medical doctor and bioengineer

Ken Money, physiologist researching motion sickness with NASA

Bjarni Tryggvason, physicist and pilot instructor

Other training in the air pressure chamber included a sudden low drop in air pressure, something that might happen in an emergency on board the space shuttle. This allowed them to practice putting on oxygen masks.

Part of the Canadian astronaut's job has always been to teach the public about space and Canada's role in space research. Roberta and her colleagues had a lot to learn. They read all they could about space and Canadian research and technology. A few months after accepting the job, they were giving talks about space all across the country. They also visited NASA at the Kennedy Space Center in Florida, to learn some of the ropes. Marc Garneau was the first Canadian to fly in space, in Mission 41–G aboard the space shuttle *Challenger*, October 5–13, 1984.

Roberta was there to greet the crew when they came back down to Earth. She thought Garneau looked terrific, "beaming all over." She also noticed that "They didn't smell half as bad as they said they were going to." After showers and a screen by NASA doctors, Roberta ran tests on Garneau and another astronaut. The experiments were designed to look at the effect

Part of the Canadian astronaut's job has always been to teach the public about space and Canada's role in space research.

of space on the human body before their bodies got used to Earth's gravity again.

Following Garneau's mission, work continued for the six Canadian astronauts. Over the years, there were many public appearances and many media interviews. Roberta also continued to study the effects of low gravity on the human body. Part of her work was to help design experiments to be carried out in space later—not just in physiology, but also in other branches of biology.

Roberta began working with scientists across Canada to plan useful space experiments, and she continued to broaden her knowledge and expertise in ways that would benefit an astronaut on shuttle missions. For example, she and her fellow astronauts took a geology course designed just for them, to teach them how to identify Earth's features from space. There were other courses in astronomy, oceanography, and photography.

A Tragic Reversal of Plans

The next astronaut chosen for a mission was Steve MacLean, whose mission was scheduled for 1987. Roberta was still waiting and hoping that one day she'd be chosen for a mission, too. Then, tragedy struck. In 1986, the space shuttle *Challenger* exploded shortly after liftoff and all the crew members were killed. MacLean's mission was put on hold—indefinitely. The *Challenger* disaster was very upsetting to the public, particularly as millions of people, including school children, watched its launch on television and saw the explosion.

NASA was devastated, and the entire space shuttle program was suspended. A major investigation into the accident was ordered and big changes were made in the way space missions were run to make sure that safety was always put first. It was almost three years before the space shuttle program started again.

At the time of the *Challenger* disaster, Roberta thought carefully about continuing as an astronaut. She felt tremendous uncertainty about when, or even if, she'd get to go into space, and she needed to consider her long-term career goals. She had already given up a great deal. When she had become an astronaut in 1983, she still thought she'd like to have children, and she imagined she could be in the space program for several years, then quit and have a family. That life path no longer seemed realistic in 1986, and she had to think carefully

Then, tragedy struck. In 1986, the space shuttle Challenger *exploded shortly after liftoff and all the crew members were killed.*

about what was next in life. Was she prepared to continue waiting? If so, for how long?

With the risks involved in space travel made obvious by the *Challenger* disaster, Roberta was also considering what impact her astronaut ambitions would have on her family. Her father had died a few months earlier, and she did not want to put her family through more grief.

Roberta did not quit; none of the six original Canadian astronauts quit. Instead, she renewed her love of medical research. Roberta started a study to determine the effects of microgravity (very weak gravity) on blood flow in the brain. Not only could this research help astronauts who spend time in space, but it could also help people on Earth who suffer from changes in blood flow in the brain—such as stroke patients. Roberta's partners in this research were the Toronto General Hospital, Ryerson Polytechnical Institute (now Ryerson Polytechnic University), and the Johnson Space Center.

One of the questions Roberta hoped to answer in her research was whether the shift in fluids in the body when a person first enters space has any effect on the blood in the brain. She used a method to measure the speed of blood flow in the arteries in the brain involving ultrasound. Some of her experiments took place on the KC–135—NASA's training airplane that flies up and down like a roller coaster. On the down ride, astronauts inside experience low gravity—just like in space, except it only lasts for 20–30 seconds. In a two- to three-hour flight, astronauts feel what it is like to have low gravity on the down ride, and extra gravity on the up ride. This happens over and over again, 40–50 times in one flight.

Roberta's results from the KC–135 experiments suggested that microgravity does cause a decrease in blood flow in the brain. Roberta kept the goal of her research focused on two things. She wanted not just to increase understanding of the effect of space on the body but also to help scientists "understand a bit more about some of the basic physiological things that are going on normally in you and me just walking around."

During this time, the Soviet Union's space agency asked Roberta to join a mission to the space station. They wanted to examine the effects of space on women. Roberta declined. She wanted to go to space as an astronaut, not as a test subject.

In 1990, more than eight years after joining the space program, Roberta learned that she was finally selected to go on a NASA mission. There was, again, the question of whether she was given the job instead of one of the other astronauts because she was a woman. Roberta was upset by this idea. She vowed she would quit if that were the case, and she pointed out that choosing her because she was female would be a foolish thing for her employers to do:

"...it would be the worst thing to have a woman selected for this flight just because she's a woman...the best person must be selected because otherwise you end up with egg on your face."

Of course, anything could happen to delay the schedule but, with a mission assignment in hand, Roberta was one step closer to getting off Earth.

NASA's KC–135 has another name: the Vomit Comet. This is not an official name, but a nickname given to the aircraft by its passengers. Weightlessness can make people feel sick to their stomach, and a ride on the KC–135 gives passengers a taste of both microgravity and the nausea that goes with it. Everyone who flies in the KC–135 is given a plastic vomit bag.

In this photo, a group of astronauts is subjected to 20–30 seconds of weightlessness during one of the maneuvers performed by the KC–135 aircraft.

THE VOMIT COMET

The Boeing KC–135A (later called the Vomit Comet when used by NASA to train astronauts) is shown during a test flight in 1979.

Chapter 3
Mission STS–42

O nce the seven crew members were chosen for the first shuttle mission to carry the International Microgravity Laboratory (IML), more than a year of training began.

NASA Training

Each of the crew had specialized skills and particular responsibilities. The commander, Ronald Grabe, was the leader. He was assisted by the pilot, Stephen Oswald, and the flight engineer, William Readdy. Known as the orbiter crew, these three men had the job of operating the shuttle.

The two mission specialists selected were Sonny Carter and Norman Thagard. They were responsible for maintaining the orbiter and IML equipment. Finally were the payload specialists, who were responsible for running

Once chosen, Roberta regularly spent time with NASA at the Space Centers in Houston, Florida, and Alabama working with the STS–42 crew.

the experiments. Roberta Bondar, of the Canadian Space Agency, was in charge of the life science experiments, and Ulf Merbold, a West German astronaut with the European Space Agency, was in charge of the physics experiments.

Once chosen, Roberta regularly spent time with NASA at the Space Centers in Houston, Florida, and Alabama working with the STS–42 crew. She also spent a great deal of time jetting around the world to meet with the 200 researchers whose experiments she would be conducting. She practiced over and over again using the equipment of the IML, and she had to learn some science in fields that were not her greatest strengths, such as crystal formation.

A large part of training for space is about safety. The procedures an astronaut must perform should anything go wrong in space are practiced over and over so that the actions will be automatic in a real emergency. For example, if the solid rocket boosters stop working before enough power is generated to shoot the shuttle into orbit, the astronauts inside must escape. To escape before liftoff, astronauts must lock their visors down, pull a green knob, pull the quick-disconnect lap seatbelts, release their parachutes, leave the shuttle, and slide down the wire to the launch pad.

If astronauts have to escape after liftoff, they must keep their parachutes on when they leave the shuttle. In case they land in water after escaping a shuttle, astronauts practice jumping into water with their 90-pound (41 kg) suits. They also practice survival methods for staying in the water for days at a time.

Mission STS–42 crewmates Roberta Bondar and Steve Oswald work in the IML (International Microgravity Laboratory) as part of the mission's study of the effects of low gravity on humans.

"How many Canadians do you think I'm carrying on my shoulders? But they don't weigh anything in space..."

Roberta Bondar, on the importance of her space mission to Canadians

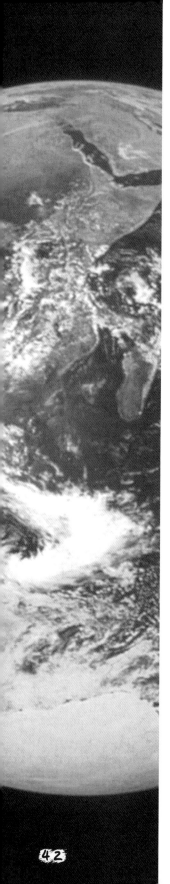

Roberta found this part of training fun. It is a good thing, too, as astronauts in mission training are not allowed any risky hobbies, such as skydiving, for example. An astronaut has to satisfy her need for excitement somehow and, in Roberta's case, what better way than training for emergency escapes?

About six months before liftoff, training intensified, and the astronauts were required to be focused on the mission and nothing else. There was little opportunity for time off. Workdays were long, and there was plenty of studying to do in the evenings.

Setbacks and Delays

For each crew member chosen, there is always a backup astronaut chosen who went through the same training. Should something go wrong, the backup would be able to step in with a moment's notice. For example, if the pilot caught the flu prior to liftoff, he would not be able to go on the mission and his backup would take his place. For Mission STS–42, a tragedy occurred in April 1991, after the team of seven had already been training together for over a year. Mission specialist Sonny Carter was killed in a commercial plane crash. The crew members were devastated, but the mission continued with David Hilmers taking his place. The crew dedicated Mission STS–42 to the memory of Sonny Carter.

There would be more setbacks during the preparations for Mission STS–42, including a total of 19 delays. The shuttle that was planned to carry the crew and the IML also changed several times. Originally, the *Columbia* space

The International Microgravity Laboratory

Every flight into space has a purpose. The purpose of STS–42, Roberta's *Discovery* space flight, was to do scientific experiments about the effects of microgravity. The equipment for a mission is located in the long part of the shuttle, which is equivalent to the part of a plane where passengers sit or cargo is carried. This is called the payload—this is what is "paying" for the flight. The payload on STS–42 mission was the International Microgravity Laboratory (IML), a module that was attached to the crew module by a tunnel.

Inside the laboratory was a wide range of equipment and supplies to do many experiments. The air within the IML was controlled much as it is on an airplane, so an astronaut did not have to wear a space suit while inside. The IML had a work bench and racks for the experiments. The IML was also designed with air-lock compartments so that experiments could be exposed to outer space and then brought back into the laboratory for the astronaut to take measurements or make changes.

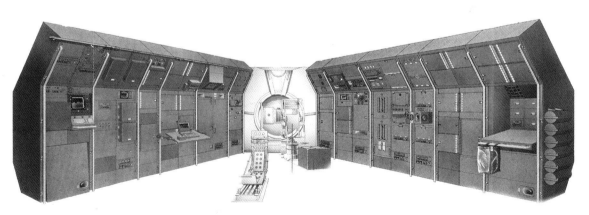

This diagram shows the interior of the IML as it would appear if it were spread open, like a fan. In reality, the lab is quite narrow.

shuttle was to carry them, but NASA decided to change how *Columbia* was used. In 1991, NASA took *Columbia* out of the space flight schedule to change the quarters and equipment to make it suitable for longer missions. *Discovery* was the shuttle next in line for the flight, but it could only fly for a seven-day mission, not a ten-day one. So the mission's length was changed to seven days. Then, *Discovery* was found to be in need of repair— cracked hinges made it unsuitable for space flight.

Mission STS–42 was rescheduled to fly on the shuttle *Atlantis*. This shuttle, too, was found to have problems—fuel leaks. All space flights scheduled for *Atlantis* were canceled. Meanwhile, the cracked hinges on *Discovery* had been repaired, and it was now ready to go. So the mission was put on *Discovery*, and that meant the experiments that had been planned for ten days of orbit had to be squeezed into a seven-day schedule. It would be a very busy week.

"You can do or be anything you want to. Expect success, not failure."

Sonny Carter, who died before he could go on Mission STS–42

Space Rehearsals

In the months before liftoff, the STS–42 crew participated in simulated missions, called *sims* for short by the astronauts. These lasted up to 48 hours. They gave the crew a chance to work together in a closed space and also to practice the tasks they would be doing

In case astronauts wind up in the ocean after an emergency, they need to practice using their survival gear, such as the personal inflatable boat, shown here, in which Roberta is riding.

160 miles (258 km) up in the air. A large water tank was used to create conditions resembling low gravity to give the astronauts some experience in working beyond the gravitational pull of Earth.

Everything is different in space, so astronauts have a lot to learn. NASA even has a simulated "space toilet." Going to the bathroom in space is not as easy as it is on Earth, because everything that comes out of the body floats. That can get rather messy. The shuttle's waste disposal system uses a vacuum to suck up waste as it leaves the body and put it into a container for disposal. New astronauts are provided with practice before they leave the ground. NASA calls the experience "potty training."

Other shuttle training includes practice using the foot straps that line the "floor" of the shuttle. The straps help give astronauts footing so they can work at a bench or do other tasks without drifting around freely. Housecleaning, packing, cooking, and learning how to use the cameras are all part of the job. By the time astronauts reach space, they have gone through the motions of doing just about everything they need to do up there—as well as on the way up and the way back down. Simulated missions also give astronauts a chance to solve problems that might come up during a mission. Being prepared can save time and lives.

It isn't just the astronauts who practice during simulated missions—the ground control crew does as well. Getting a shuttle into orbit and back down again is very much a team effort, and it takes many NASA staff working behind the scenes to make a mission a success. Everyone needs to rehearse.

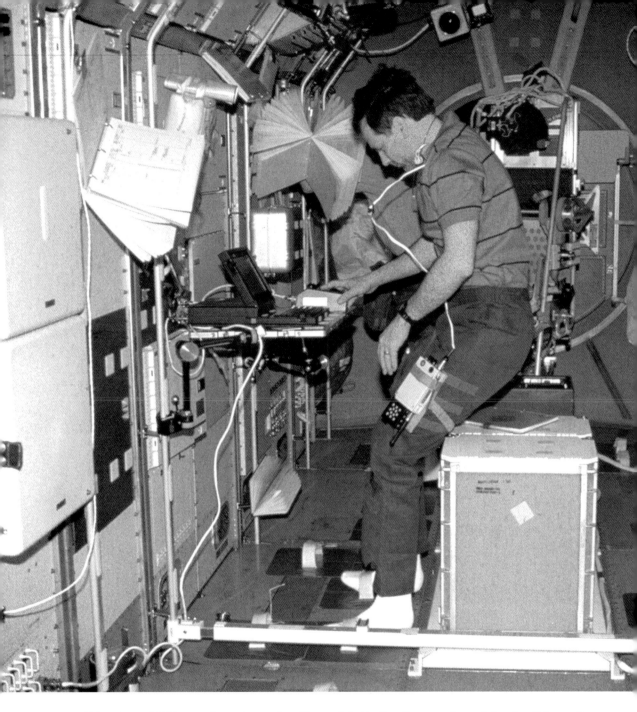

Mission STS–42 Commander Ronald J. Grabe works with the Mental Workload and Performance Experiment (MWPE) in the International Microgravity Laboratory (IML). This experiment was designed as a result of difficulties experienced by crew members working at a computer station on an earlier space shuttle mission.

Out of This World

Space is an alien environment. There is no water, no weather, and no air. Beyond Earth's atmosphere, there is nothing between the shuttle and the Sun's rays, and the radiation levels are fatal. So are the temperatures. When the shuttle is in orbit on the side of Earth in line with the Sun, the temperatures are as hot as 250°F (121°C), and when on the other side of Earth, away from the Sun, as low as -150°F (-65°C). These conditions are uninhabitable for humans and all earthly life as we know it.

Gravity gives objects weight. It holds them against the planet, and our bodies are adapted to develop and live in it. Without it, the rules change.

The space shuttle is like a miniature, artificial Earth inside an aluminum shell. Inside this shell, temperature, air pressure, oxygen levels, water, food, and energy are all created to mimic the conditions on Earth. There is one major aspect of living on Earth, however, that is not replicated in the shuttle, and that is Earth's gravity. Gravity gives objects weight. It holds them against the planet, and our bodies are adapted to develop and live in it. Without it, the rules change. Accomplishing tasks that are simple on Earth—like moving from one place to another, closing drawers, eating a can of peaches, or lying in bed and reading a book— are at best interesting and at worst incredibly difficult. Existence in the space shuttle is complex and marvelous.

After Roberta's first glorious view of Earth through *Discovery*'s windows, she set to work— with only seven days, and every minute counting. First, the flight chairs were taken down and stowed. The astronauts changed out of their LES suits and put them away. This was the crew's first taste of attempting a task that is easy on Earth, but not so easy in space. The clothes floated and they unfolded themselves. When a locker door was opened, the clothes inside floated out of it! This is the down side of wearing clothes in space. One up side is that astronauts on the shuttle can put both legs into their pants at once.

The first day's responsibilities for the STS–42 crew included getting the shuttle equipment working. The fuel cells needed to be started. They produce electricity by combining hydrogen and oxygen, and they create drinkable water in the process. Lights, air systems, communication systems, and the waste disposal unit (the official name for the space toilet) must all be "switched on." Roberta's job the first day also entailed setting up the IML. At two hours after launch, the doors of the payload bay were opened to release the heat the engines produced during liftoff. The payload bay doors were important for maintaining the temperature of the IML.

In addition to the official crew patch for Mission STS–42, each crew member was given a personal patch. Roberta Bondar's patch featured several personal touches, including an outline of Roberta's native Great Lakes region and a space shuttle "morphing" into the Canadian maple leaf.

By rolling the shuttle away from the Sun into the dark of space, the payload bay and the IML were cooled. Rolling the shuttle toward the Sun warmed up the payload bay and IML.

All of this work was done while the astronauts' bodies were adjusting to space. The first several hours of space tend to make people feel ill. Some of the crew experienced nausea and vomiting. They did not stop their work, though; they were trained to function in poor conditions. They did, however, carry plastic vomit bags in their pockets. Over the first six to ten hours, the crew got puffy faces as the fluid collected in their upper bodies, without gravity to hold it down. Over this period of time, the kidneys handled the excess fluid and the astronauts ended the first day with less fluid and less blood flowing through their veins than when they started. With less fluid to pump, their hearts shrank in size!

While the adjustments to space living were uncomfortable, there were some extraordinary experiences as well. For one, the shuttle was

THE BLUE PLANET

Many who see Earth from space are amazed by its color. Next to the black backdrop of the Universe, Earth is bright blue, with swirls of white clouds that give it the appearance of a marble. The blue color comes from Earth's atmosphere or, to be more specific, the predominant molecules in that atmosphere—nitrogen and oxygen. These gas molecules are smaller than the wavelengths of visible light. Light from the Sun is made up of the colors of the rainbow, which appear white when mixed together.

Blue is the shortest of the visible wavelengths. When light from the Sun hits Earth's atmosphere, the short wavelengths bounce off the molecules of nitrogen and oxygen, scatter, and we see blue. Molecules of water vapor and dust, which form clouds in the atmosphere, are larger than the wavelengths of visible light. When light from the Sun hits these molecules, all of the colors of the rainbow bounce off them, and we see white.

circling Earth very quickly, traveling at more than 17,000 miles per hour (27,359 KPH). At this speed it took about ten minutes to pass over North America, and the shuttle circled Earth 19 times every day. In their first hour and a half, the crew members of STS–42 witnessed both a sunset and sunrise—from a lookout point that provided an amazing view of Earth, the Sun, and the Moon.

The Necessities of Life

On Day 03 of Mission STS–42, Commander Ron Grabe discovered an unexpected plastic bag floating among the crew. Everyone recognized it. It was a bag of sandwiches they been given by NASA staff to eat during the launch. In all the excitement, it had not been touched and had been forgotten. The floating bag was swollen and round. It had puffed up with gas created by bacteria. The astronauts knew that bacteria grow faster and bigger in space, so they didn't touch those sandwiches! Instead, the bag was put in the trash, which on a space shuttle means to put it in a plastic bag and attach it to the sides of the shuttle with duct tape somewhere out of the way. Roberta joked, "We need one of those creatures from *Star Wars* who gobbles the trash."

The mid-deck of the orbiter contained food lockers, storage, the washroom facilities, the sleeping compartments, and a small appliance to warm up meals. It was a crowded place! The food each astronaut had to eat was chosen from the NASA menu well ahead of time. There were many choices, but no baked beans or broccoli.

HOW TO EAT IN SPACE

To eat a freeze-dried meal, STS–42 astronauts followed these steps:
1. Poke a hole in the food package.
2. Inject the right amount of hot or cold water.
3. Shake the pack until the water and food inside are evenly mixed.
4. Make an opening in the pack with scissors big enough for a spoon.
5. Use the spoon to try to get the food to your mouth.

Roberta reported that cookies were her favorite treat in space. In this photo, she is either making a genuine effort to manage her microgravity snack, or she is using low gravity as an excuse to play with her food!

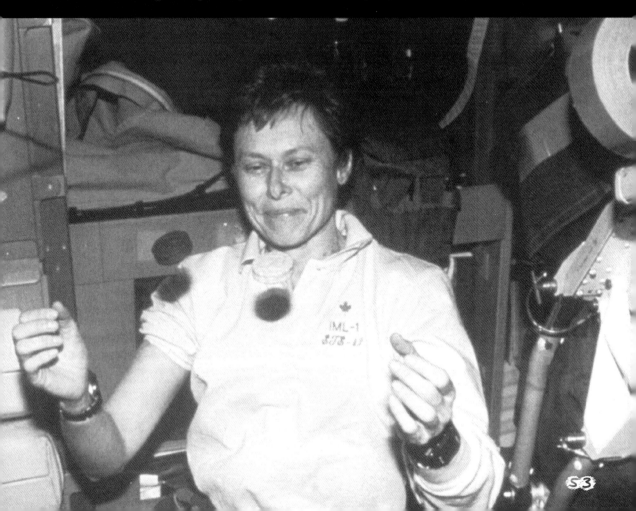

These foods might give an astronaut gas, which could cause pain in the abdomen, and that might be dangerous.

NASA's freeze-dried meals were stored in individually wrapped packages. A small heater warmed up the food. For snacks, there were cans of pudding, yogurt, and applesauce, which

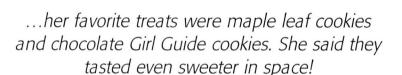

...her favorite treats were maple leaf cookies and chocolate Girl Guide cookies. She said they tasted even sweeter in space!

were attached to the walls of the food area with duct tape. These cans had pull-tabs on them, like many canned snacks in grocery stores. In fact, it was NASA engineers who invented this pull-tab! Tortillas with a jar of cheese sauce and a packet of salsa were on Roberta's menu, and her favorite treats were maple leaf cookies and chocolate Girl Guide cookies. She said they tasted even sweeter in space!

Eating had its challenges, but the astronauts all had Velcro, which they used for all kinds of things, including sticking a food tray to their pants. Most of the astronauts' food stayed attached to the spoon easily—water is sticky in microgravity. Because food sticks to a spoon in space, rather than resting on top of it, a spoonful of Roberta's space food was more like a dipstick—with her food sticking to all sides. Still, Roberta had some difficulty with some shrimp cocktail sauce that floated away. She had to warn her crewmates, "The sauce is loose!" Having food loose is not a good thing, as it can damage the experiments or the equipment.

Hot and cold water for making drinks was available to Roberta, too, and there were plenty of juice packs. The only way to drink in space is to use a straw. Even coffee or hot chocolate must be sucked up. Space straws have a special closure on them, however, to stop the liquid from moving up the straw and floating into the air. Astronauts amuse themselves by letting a drop of juice escape from the straw of their juice pack. The drop forms a perfect, floating sphere, which an astronaut can suck up with a straw or, if it is small enough, swallow whole.

More Necessities

Exercise was another necessity of life on the shuttle. Without gravity, muscles deteriorate, and so do bones. To keep muscle and bone loss to a minimum, the astronauts exercised. On Mission STS–42, a specially-designed rowing machine was tried out. As of 2009, the main piece of exercise equipment on board *Discovery* was a stationary bicycle.

Keeping clean was also tricky without a way to keep water in place. Roberta and her crewmates wiped themselves with a wet towel instead of having a shower. Soapy water was supplied in packs. It was put on the skin with

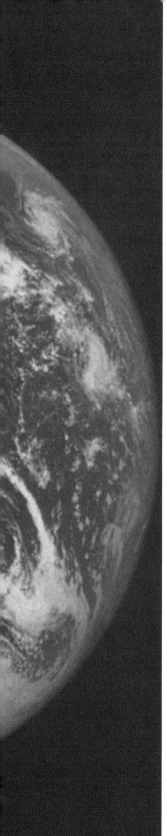

a towel, and taken off with another wet towel. Going to the bathroom involved being strapped down—literally! Roberta had to attach foot and thigh straps to keep from floating away while sitting on the toilet.

Astronauts cannot lie in bed to sleep while in space, so there were no beds on the shuttle. Instead, Roberta climbed into a compartment that looked a little bit like a locker on its side. Inside was a kind of thin sleeping bag with straps to keep her in. She shut the door and put in ear plugs to block out noise from the mid-deck. Astronauts select music and recordings to listen to while in "presleep" or during off time. Roberta brought with her the theme song from *Star Wars Return of the Jedi*, as well as "O Canada" and "The Star-Spangled Banner," some Girl Guide songs, recordings of her family, and more.

Work

The work, meal, and sleep times of every astronaut were carefully planned and scheduled—in as little as five-minute intervals. The STS–42 crew was divided into two 12-hour shifts—the red shift and the blue shift. While one shift was working, the other was sleeping. Roberta got the day shift—she was happy about this, as it meant her family did not have to stay up to watch her on television!

Roberta and the other specialists worked long and hard on the experiments. Because of the tight timelines—the ten days of planned experiments squashed into seven days—the entire crew was involved. This was highly unusual; normally only payload specialists performed experiments. STS–42 was an especially effective team, however, and their commander felt it was important that they all contribute. Roberta and the others sometimes worked 16 hours, not 12, in the beginning days of the mission, to accomplish all the tasks on their schedule.

While working, the crew was in close contact with the ground crew, giving them information about everything that was happening. The payload specialist backups were hard at work on the ground, too. They were in contact with Roberta and Merbold minute by minute. They provided assistance and advice and received instructions from the scientists on Earth about what to do next in the experiments. Roberta's work involved setting up lights and equipment, such as microscopes for experiments, and taking them down and putting them away again. She planted seeds and moved containers in and out of space. All her work was done in a very crowded space with objects that floated away if given the chance.

Part of every shuttle crew's work is to record the mission with many different cameras. An IMAX video camera with an astronaut camera crew recorded Mission STS–42 as well as the view from the shuttle. The IMAX movie *Destiny in Space* was the result. Photographs of every description provided spectacular images of our planet as well as valuable information about geography, weather, and agriculture. All of the crew were able to use many cameras to take photographs when they were not working. Roberta was particularly attracted to this task:

> *"Each second from space grants me a new wonder and a new chance to capture forever on film the endearing landscape below, which looks like a painting or a tapestry."*

There were times on the mission when Roberta's crewmates needed to encourage her to leave the window and the camera to eat lunch or get some sleep.

Taking pictures from space can be challenging. A moving camera makes for a blurry picture, and the cameras in the shuttle floated. So did the photographers. Getting everything to stay still took energy. In addition, any floating food particles or dust in the shuttle stuck to the windows, which made the windows hard to keep clean. Furthermore, the shuttle was moving quickly, so any point on Earth was only in view for a moment. So when Roberta wanted to take a photo of the Great Lakes, for instance, she had to be ready and waiting.

Another task the astronauts shared was conducting press conferences to talk to people on Earth. The president of the United States called the crew, and the prime minister of Canada called Roberta, too. Former astronauts and school children connected directly with the mission via satellite. On Day 04 of Mission STS–42, the crew received some excellent news.

IMAX TECHNOLOGY

In the 1960s, three Canadians—Graeme Ferguson, Robert Kerr, and Roman Kroitor—developed the technology to produce giant-screen movies. They called their technology and their company IMAX. The first IMAX film was shown in 1970. There have been more than a hundred others since. IMAX cameras film in higher resolution, so the film looks crisp and clear on a screen that is ten times the size of a normal screen. There are permanent IMAX theaters all over the world. Tens of millions of people have visited them to watch the nine movies filmed in space aboard shuttle missions, including STS–42.

SATELLITES AND COMMUNICATION

A satellite is any object that revolves around Earth. The largest satellite circling Earth is the Moon. There are also many artificial satellites put in orbit on purpose, most them launched to aid in communication. The first artificial satellite, called *Sputnik 1*, circled Earth in 1951. It was launched by the government of the former Soviet Union. For a long time, satellites were very specialized pieces of equipment owned by the military. Some satellites were used to spy on other countries. Now, by one estimate, there are as many as 25,000. (Not all of them work!) We use satellites to watch the weather, tell us our position (GPS), access the Internet, and talk to each other on our cell phones. All satellites get into space in one of two ways: They are attached to a rocket and blasted into orbit, or they ride inside a NASA shuttle payload bay.

Things were going so well that their mission was extended one day—so they would be in space eight days instead of seven. The eighth day was spent extending the experiments to obtain even more information about how space affects living things.

STS-42 Experiments

Roberta and Merbold were in charge of 42 experiments developed by 200 researchers from 13 different countries. Everything from the human body to crystals was tested to determine the effect of space. Two main factors associated with space were of interest—microgravity and radiation from the Sun. The 42 experiments all had names. For example, the Mental Workload and Performance Experiment (MPWE) tested a new workstation/computer design for astronauts to do their work.

In the Critical Point Facility experiment, various fluids were heated in small test containers to the point at which they changed into a gas, like heating water on the stove until it boils and turns into steam. On Earth, the gas from a boiling liquid rises while the fluid stays behind—because of gravity. Scientists wanted to know what would happen to the gas in space—would it form a bubble in the middle of the test cell and push the fluid out to the sides? The Critical Point Facility experiment demonstrated that this is not what happens.

Photographs taken by special equipment showed that gas escaping from a fluid in space forms many bubbles throughout the fluid. The researchers who developed this experiment back home on Earth applauded with excitement

STS–42 mission specialist David C. Hilmers participates in an experiment to determine how people respond to changing stimuli from the environment. This test requires that the subject be strapped into a chair that rotates in many directions. The subject is wearing a helmet that covers the eyes. The experiment measures which parts of the nervous system are called upon to help us interpret sensory information in low gravity and other extreme conditions.

when the photos of the bubbles were beamed down by satellite.

Roberta was also responsible for growing some crystals. Previous missions had demonstrated that crystals grow larger, faster, and with fewer defects in space. In the IML, Roberta grew crystals, such as mercury iodide, which look like solid chunks of bright red strawberry jelly. They were to be used in nuclear power plants. Other crystals were grown to be used in telescopes, to treat cancer, or to study protein structures.

The effects of space were tested on organisms other than humans, including frog eggs, fruit flies, hamsters, slime molds, stick insects, bacteria, mouse cells, nematode worms, yeast, and plants such as wheat, oats, and lentils. Some questions asked about the plants were these: How much more do they grow with little gravity? Do the roots grow down? Do plants move their leaves toward light in the same way if there is little gravity?

There were many experiments that asked questions about the effect of microgravity on the human body. The role of gravity in the balancing system of the inner ear and the eyes was one aspect of Roberta's work in the IML. To perform this study, Roberta strapped herself, or her crewmates, into a high-tech chair with a helmet over the eyes. The chair was spun around and put on its side and turned in circles.

Measurements were recorded of how the eye responded to these tests. The results of this experiment demonstrated that over the course of a week in space, the human body relies more and more over time on information from the eye to determine its position and stay balanced, rather than information from the inner ear.

The Venous Compliance and Experimental Anti-Gravity Suit was an experiment to test the design of a new anti-gravity suit. Astronauts wear anti-gravity suits inside their orange LES suits because their body fluids are pulled back into their legs during re-entry. This is the opposite of what happens when the fluid rises to the top of the body when the astronauts first arrive in space.

...the results of their experiments made Mission STS–42 one of the most successful in the history of the space shuttle program.

The anti-gravity suit inflates with air around the legs, preventing too much fluid from collecting there, and instead keeping it in the upper body and the brain. The new design tested on Mission STS–42 was found to be more effective than previous designs.

The cooperation of Roberta and the rest of the crew, the amount of information they were able to collect in a short period of time, and the results of their experiments made Mission STS–42 one of the most successful in the history of the space shuttle program.

western union

WESTAR VI

64

CANADA IN SPACE

Canada's presence in space has extended beyond its astronauts' participation. Canadian engineers were involved in the development of numerous NASA spacecraft, including those in the Mercury, Gemini, Apollo, and space shuttle programs. Canada has always been a world leader in building advanced communications satellites, but perhaps its best-known contribution to the NASA space program is the building of a robotic arm for the shuttle. Called the Canadarm, this technological marvel manipulates objects—including satellites, telescopes, and solar panels.

Canada's contribution to space engineering has continued with its involvement in the International Space Station (ISS). The ISS is a research laboratory in orbit that has been in continuous operation since 2000. It will be used until at least 2020, perhaps longer. There are always astronauts living in the Space Station, although none permanently. They spend about four to six months before spacecraft, such as the shuttle, bring new astronauts to replace them and bring them home. Canadarm2 has been the major robotic arm used on the Space Station to manipulate objects. Its tasks include assembling the structure of the station itself. A smaller Canadian robot with two arms, called Dextre, has been used to do smaller jobs that at one time only an astronaut in a space suit could do.

Opposite: The Canadarm is shown on the job during space shuttle Mission STS -41B in February 1984. Here, the Canadarm is below and behind an astronaut who is using it as a platform from which he is doing work while on a spacewalk.

Chapter 4
Down to Earth

At the end of the eighth day in space, the Mission STS–42 crew began to make preparations for the trip home. This is not a simple process. Every single object loose in the shuttle needed to be tucked away where it could do no harm to equipment or people—about 1,000 objects in all.

Shutting Things Down

One of these objects was Roberta's eyeglasses. She was surprised to come across them floating loose in the mid-deck. She'd forgotten all about them! For unknown reasons, vision improves in space, and Roberta had taken her glasses off when she found she didn't need them anymore. Luckily, she found them again before the trip home began.

Mission Control at the Johnson Space Center in Houston gave the go-ahead to start the procedure to re-enter Earth's atmosphere with the words "go for deorbit burn."

All the equipment, in addition to being put away, had to be deactivated. All the experiments, except for one, had to be halted. Roberta and mission specialist David Hilmers volunteered to have their blood pressure and heart rate monitored during the entire journey home. They would take measurements on each other while in their chairs on the mid-deck. To prepare for the journey, the tunnel that the astronauts had been using to get from the mid-deck to the Spacelab was sealed off. The payload bay doors were closed and secured. A few hours before starting the journey home, the flight chairs were reassembled.

During this time, the astronauts also needed to prepare their bodies for the return to Earth. They had less blood and fluid at the end of the mission than they did when they started, and they needed to increase their fluids to be able to function well on Earth. So they started drinking lots of fluids. An hour before re-entry, they drank four to eight drink packs each. They also took salt tablets, because salt helps the body keep water in the tissues. The astronauts kept drinking and eating salt tablets during the journey as much as they could. Without these precautions, astronauts returning to Earth can feel very dizzy, as well as thirsty.

At about one hour before re-entry, the crew put on their LES suits, the same orange ones they wore on their trip into orbit. This time, they had no one except each other to help put them on. It was a little easier, however, in their low-gravity environment, as the suits barely weighed anything.

Crew members on the day shift of Mission STS–42 float as they talk to folks back home via satellite. This picture is a still from the 1994 IMAX movie Destiny in Space, *which used photos and footage from Roberta's shuttle mission as the basis of a documentary on space travel.*

The Journey Home

With everybody strapped in securely,
Commander Grabe and Pilot Oswald checked
the computers and flight systems. It was 20
minutes until the engines fired, and the crew
members were in the dark—it was night time.
Mission Control at the Johnson Space Center
in Houston gave the go-ahead to start the
procedure to re-enter Earth's atmosphere with
the words "go for deorbit burn." The shuttle
was moved into re-entry position, with its
nose pointed at an angle toward Earth,
and the orbiter's engines were fired.

*The shuttle had to descend gently and land
in a particular spot...There was only
one chance to get it right.*

The engines only burned for a few minutes.
It does not take much power to bring the
shuttle back down to Earth; gravity does the
work. In reality, the shuttle fell to the ground.
It was still a tricky business, however. The
shuttle had to descend gently and land in a
particular spot, in this case on Edwards Air
Force Base in California's Mojave Desert.
There was only one chance to get it right.

Computers largely controlled the first part of
the shuttle descent. Roberta and the rest of the

crew felt a gentle nudge pulling them against their seats—this was the only indication they were moving—although the force of gravity increased as they moved closer to home. In less than 30 minutes, the shuttle reached Earth's atmosphere. Just before hitting the atmosphere, the STS–42 astronauts inflated their gravity pants to prevent too much of their blood from being pulled by gravity into their legs, away from their hearts and their brains.

Discovery's crew members knew when they hit the atmosphere—the friction made the orbiter vibrate. For the first time in over a week, there was noise—the rushing of air, which got louder and louder. The shuttle experienced immense heat and became engulfed in a fiery glow, just as a meteorite becomes a "shooting star" when it hits the atmosphere and bursts into flames. The astronauts inside were protected by heat-resistant tiles covering the orbiter. The intense heat was caused by air molecules getting hit by the heavy, fast-moving object and being compressed very quickly.

This effect is a normal part of re-entry, and the friction of the shuttle hitting the air also caused it to slow down gradually from its orbiting speed of 25 times the speed of sound. The shuttle slowed down with a series of turns and curves, a little bit like a skier does on her way downhill. Each time the shuttle turned at an angle with one wing pointing down and then flew in a curve, it dropped closer to Earth, as if

The shuttle experienced immense heat and became engulfed in a fiery glow, just as a meteorite becomes a "shooting star" when it hits the atmosphere and bursts into flames.

it was cutting through a layer of air.

As the shuttle descended closer to Earth and slowed down, the crew members felt as if they were in turbulence. The shuttle was shaking, and they experienced more and more force on their bodies. At its peak, the force was twice the force of gravity, or 2G. Since they were used to being weightless, however, they felt this force even more. It did not hurt, but it felt uncomfortable. At about two minutes before landing, the shuttle neared the speed of sound, known as Mach 1.

When the shuttle reached this speed, the family and friends gathered on the ground heard two loud booms—the first was the nose of the shuttle breaking the sound barrier. The second was the tail breaking the sound barrier. The shuttle slowed to less than Mach 1, and

WHERE TO LAND THE SHUTTLE?

The prime location for landing a shuttle is the same place they are launched: the Kennedy Space Center in Florida. However, sometimes weather does not cooperate and visibility is poor or the landing runway is wet. Then, the shuttle lands in the backup location at Edwards Air Force Base in California. If an emergency landing needs to be made, there are shuttle landing runways available around the world including Australia, Canada, France, Germany, Spain, Ireland, Iceland, Saudi Arabia, Gambia, Turkey, and numerous locations across the United States. Only one other runway besides the Kennedy Space Center and Edwards Air Force Base was ever used to land a shuttle: White Sands Space Harbor in New Mexico.

the glowing stopped. At this point, the commander and pilot took over control of the shuttle from the computers. The astronauts' friends and family saw the shuttle come into view and cheered.

Another Critical Moment

The landing was a tense moment, at least for the audience. No shuttle has the power to circle around and try a landing again. Commander Grabe and Pilot Oswald had to get it right the first time. In addition, the many experiments and specimens on board required a soft landing. Shuttle pilots are among the best of the best. Not only had every shuttle landing been successful, but there was a tradition to be followed: the landing wheels hit the ground on the exact spot hit by the landing wheels from every previous mission.

At this point, the commander and pilot took over control of the shuttle from the computers. The astronauts' friends and family saw the shuttle come into view and cheered.

Touchdown! The wheels touched the ground and the orbiter slowed from 224 miles per hour (393 kph) with the crowd loudly cheering. It came to a stop one and a half miles (2.4 km) away.

A Disastrous Re-Entry

In 2003, over ten years after Roberta's 1992 flight, the shuttle *Columbia* and its seven-member crew re-entered Earth's atmosphere after 16 days in space. As is normal, the shuttle experienced intense heat. The heat tiles all over its belly and edges were designed to protect it from this heat and had always done so in every previous shuttle re-entry. This time, however, a tile on the left wing was damaged, and air as hot as 3,000°F (1,650°C) blew beneath *Columbia*'s tiles and surrounded the orbiter.

As the shuttle flew from California to Texas, witnesses saw a series of flashes of light in the sky. Over the next seven minutes, small parts of the shuttle fell off, leaving a trail of debris from Texas to Louisiana and Arkansas. During a good part of this time, neither ground control in Houston nor the shuttle crew were aware that anything was wrong. The shuttle was over Texas when ground control had its last communication with the crew. *Columbia* had disintegrated. There was silence.

The loss of *Columbia* and its crew was a major blow to NASA. The investigation revealed that during the shuttle's launch, a piece of foam had fallen off the external fuel tank, hit the shuttle's left wing, and damaged a heat tile. Previously, NASA had identified a problem with foam pieces coming off the external fuel tank during liftoff. They did not have a solution to the problem, however, and did not cancel the shuttle missions. As a result of the *Columbia* accident, NASA suspended the space shuttle program. It did not begin again for more than two years.

The crew members did not unbuckle their seatbelts and get out of the shuttle right away. Instead, they had a long list of procedures they had to go through first. They checked for toxic gases that might be present from unused fuel. They turned off all the equipment. They also needed a little time to get used to the weight they felt to be able to walk. They felt wobbly and unsteady, perhaps even faint.

At about one hour after landing, the crew members left the shuttle and entered the van where they changed out of their LES suits and had a drink of water—without a straw! NASA doctors checked that they were well. The van took the crew to the nearby clinic. Here, family members were waiting to greet them. More NASA doctors gave them medical tests to ensure that all was well. Roberta then underwent even more tests, as part of the experiments studying the effects of space on the human body. She finally got off work at the end of the day.

Down on the Ground

It takes a while to readjust to living in gravity. Over the course of the next week, the STS–42 astronauts noticed improvement in their balance and movement control. With gentle exercise, their hearts increased back to their normal size, and their spines, which had become as much as two inches (five cm) longer in microgravity, shrank again. There was no vacation for the astronauts after landing. For several weeks, the entire crew did numerous tests to study how

*Its drag chute deployed to slow
its landing, the space shuttle*
Discovery *touches down.*

"I need science, even more now, to help understand my relationship with this planet, which is of course not a static entity at all."

Roberta Bondar's thoughts after Mission STS–42, in *Touching the Earth*

the body readjusts after being in space. Roberta also worked with the scientists whose experiments she conducted. They went over the procedures and the results and discussed future improvements. Over the next months, Roberta and her crewmates were also hard at work giving talks to the general public about their experiences.

Within a year after Mission STS–42, Roberta quit her job as an astronaut. Her chances of going up in space again were slim. As Roberta explained:

"The main problem with space flight in my view is not the lack of ability to develop the technology to go to the Moon again, or to Mars, but rather the understanding of what physiological changes are occurring in humans."

So Roberta decided to pursue her own neurology research full-time, but on the ground. Her time in space, however, particularly her view of Earth from up there, had changed her forever.

Mission
STS–42 Facts

Fourteenth *Discovery* space shuttle flight
Forty-fifth shuttle mission overall
Launch: Jan. 22, 1992, 9:52:33 a.m. EST
Landing: Jan. 30, 1992, 8:07:17 a.m. PST
Orbits of Earth: 129
Altitude: 163 miles (262 km)
Distance traveled: 2,921,153 miles (4,701,140 km)
Duration: 8 days, 1 hour, 14 minutes, 44 seconds
Landing Speed: 229 mph (369 KPH)

The End of the Space Shuttle

The last space shuttle mission was scheduled for autumn 2010. Its purpose: to deliver spare parts to the International Space Station. After this, shuttles will no longer be used for space missions, and at the time this book was written, several of them were for sale. The original price tag was $42 million, but this was reduced to $28 million. NASA was also looking to get rid of its main shuttle engines as well. In fact, they were giving them away, though packaging and shipping charges were the responsibility of the new owner. The space shuttle *Discovery* was not sold. It was given to the Smithsonian National Air and Space Museum in Washington, D.C.

At the moment, the exact nature of the space program in the United States is undecided, and it is unclear how future astronauts will get into space. It is for certain, however, that it will not be on a shuttle!

Chapter 5
A Renaissance Woman

After leaving the Canadian Space Agency, Roberta returned to her medical research and continued to explore the effects of microgravity on the human brain. Her work led her to become a professor of space medicine at several universities, including Ryerson Polytechnic University, McMaster University, and the University of Western Ontario—all in Ontario—and the University of New Mexico.

Space Medicine
With the university of New Mexico, and NASA, Roberta led an international team for more than ten years that studied the effects of space

By understanding what happens in the brain in microgravity to cause a decrease in blood flow, Roberta and her colleagues can also help scientists understand what happens during a stroke.

on the human body. Methods that Roberta and her research team developed have been used by other neurologists. All this time, she also maintained her medical practice on a part-time basis.

Roberta's research has had several aims. Along with her colleagues, she used the KC–135 airplane (the Vomit Comet from her training days) to see how short periods of time in microgravity affect the brain and to try to figure out why. One conclusion from her work is the understanding that some people are sensitive to nausea as a result of microgravity while others are not. Those who are sensitive to nausea have blood vessels in the brain that constrict, causing a decrease in blood flow. By understanding what happens in the brain in microgravity to cause this decrease in blood flow, Roberta and her colleagues can also help scientists understand what happens during a stroke—an extreme case of reduced blood flow in the brain.

One question Roberta explored was the role a person's breathing played in reduced blood flow to the brain during periods of microgravity. The way someone breathes affects the amount of oxygen and carbon dioxide in the blood. In turn, this affects blood flow. If there is less carbon dioxide in the blood of the arteries, blood flow in the brain is reduced.

Roberta's research indicated that differences in breathing are important, but they are not enough to account for the effects of microgravity. There is more going on. Roberta also found that astronauts with an increased heart rate prior to take-off were more likely to experience

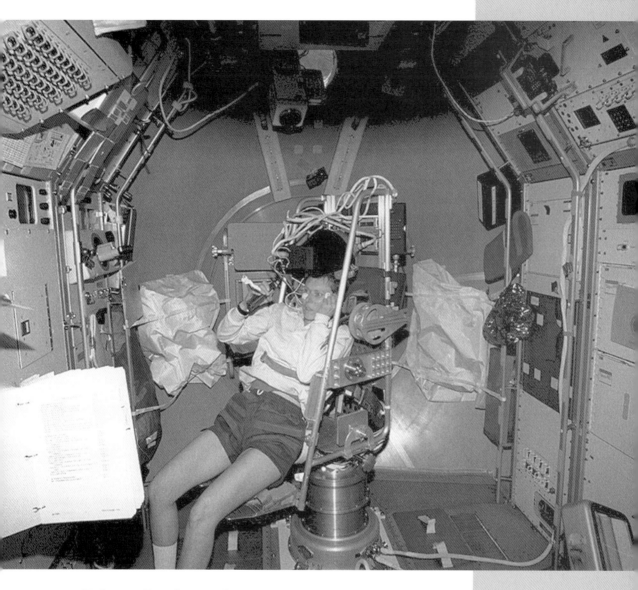

Roberta Bondar is shown in the shuttle's International Microgravity Lab (IML). She is testing the effects of head and body movements on the inner ear and balance in low gravity. In 1992, Roberta left the Canadian Space Agency to pursue her research into the effects of microgravity—on the ground.

symptoms on the day that they landed back on Earth. Also, if test subjects inhale carbon dioxide and increase its levels in their arteries, the symptoms associated with microgravity are reduced.

Astronauts who have been in space and have adapted to microgravity often experience symptoms when they recover on Earth that are similar to Parkinson's disease (shakiness, slow movement, impaired balance). Again, Roberta's space medicine research could help both astronauts and Earth-bound patients. Roberta and her colleagues found that astronauts who did suffer symptoms upon return to Earth had lower levels of a hormone called norepinephrine in their blood. This hormone is an important brain chemical that affects mood and also influences how fast the heart beats. When a person feels fear or panic, it is norepinephrine released into the blood stream that makes the heart beat faster.

Research is continuing to determine why the body reacts the way it does to microgravity. Perhaps one day this research will lead to ways to successfully treat or prevent Parkinson's disease and stroke.

"We romanticize space. It's a very difficult environment. It's very hard. It's hard on the body. But you can't beat the view."

Roberta Bondar, answering a question about what she learned in space, at a talk given to the Nova Scotia Power Company

WHAT IS A STROKE?

A stroke is a sudden loss of brain function. Most strokes happen when there is a sudden decrease in blood flow to the brain. Without oxygen or nutrients, brain cells die and no longer work. Damage from a stroke can be permanent. Signs that a person is having a stroke include numbness or weakness in parts of the body, dizziness, difficulty speaking, and severe headache. People of all ages can have a stroke, although it is much more common in older people. Stroke is the third leading cause of death in North America.

Combining Art with Science

Like other great "Renaissance men," Roberta Bondar has developed expertise in many areas. While pursuing her career as a scientist and a doctor, Roberta nurtured a serious interest in photography. The interest was always there. As a child she had a camera, and her father and uncle were both photographers. It was natural that, while in space, she would take to her job of photographing Earth through the shuttle's portholes.

The shuttle's orbit was not so far away that the entire planet was visible at once. It was more like looking at part of a giant spinning ball than at a marble. The shuttle was also close enough to capture a lot of detail—

mountains and glaciers, storms brewing over the ocean, volcanoes and craters. Roberta was overcome by the sights:

"I feel bathed in its colored light— reds, browns, greens, whites, blues. And the most beautiful of all these colors, the one that I associate with the many emotions I feel? Overwhelmingly, it is blue."

Upon her return to Earth, "the most beautiful place around," Roberta was driven to

Roberta embarked on a personal mission to photograph all of Canada's 41 national parks. The project took two and a half years and cost $2.2 million.

communicate her visions of her planet and her feelings about what she saw. She wrote a book for children about her space flight, with her sister, Barbara, who is a professional writer. It is called *On the Shuttle: Eight Days in Space.* She also wrote a book for adults called *Touching the Earth.* It features Roberta's experiences in flight, with a focus of her view of the world from "up there," as well as what the photographs of Earth taken from space can tell us.

A RENAISSANCE MAN

Calling someone a "Renaissance man" suggests they have a wide breadth of knowledge and abilities. The saying comes from changes in the culture of Europe between the 1300s and 1600s. In this period, known as the Renaissance, education, arts, science, and exploration were highly valued. This was the time in which modern science was born. The arts flourished, with advances in painting, music, theater, and literature.

It was a time when people hungry for knowledge became experts in arts as well as science, philosophy, and math. The distinctions between these subjects were not as pronounced then as they are today.

Leonardo da Vinci, the famous artist who lived in Italy in the 1500s, is a perfect example of a Renaissance man. Not only did he paint the most famous of all paintings, the *Mona Lisa*, but he also invented a glider, water pumps, and instruments of war; planned cities; and studied the physics of water, light, and movement.

No longer an astronaut, Roberta was free to pursue other interests, and she enrolled in the professional nature photography program at Brooks Institute of Photography, in Santa Barbara, California. She graduated with Honors. Roberta's photographs were first seen by the public in 1997 when Ann Thomas, a curator at the National Gallery of Canada, included some of her work in an exhibit entitled *Beauty of Another Order—Photography in Science*. A book was published with the same name.

Shortly after this exhibition, Roberta embarked on a personal mission to photograph all of Canada's 41 national parks. The project took two and a half years and cost $2.2 million. To finance it, Roberta mortgaged her house! She also received a grant from the federal government and some help from companies who sponsored her project. To get to the parks, Roberta used many methods of travel, including helicopter, Inuit sled, and foot. The resulting images were put in a book, *Passionate Vision:*

"There are very few people who would epitomize better the fusion of ancient and modern, art and science."

Helen Esmonde, Hoopers Gallery, London, UK, describing Roberta Bondar's work as a photographic artist

Discovering Canada's National Parks, which became a best seller.

Curator Ann Thomas made the stunning photographs into an art exhibit that toured across Canada. Roberta was the first person ever to photograph all of Canada's national parks. She had many adventures while doing so, with one near-death incident in the Arctic when she could have drowned. Roberta joked about it: "Nothing that dramatic happened when I was in the Space Program. We did a lot of sitting around in meetings."

A third book, *Canada: Landscape of Dreams,* was published in 2002 and features 50 of Roberta's photographs of Canada's wilderness. Each photo is accompanied by the words of famous Canadians written for the occasion. Everyone from pop stars to politicians, and artists to actors, helped Roberta to express one thing—a love of the natural world of Canada. Roberta's own words on the subject indicate her strong feelings: "I believe that there is something for everyone in this vast land to refresh both body and soul. Where else can we find heaven on Earth?"

Always the adventurer, Roberta continued to capture on film the beauty of her favorite planet, traveling the globe to do so. Photographic expeditions to the world's deserts are captured in her 2006 book, *The Arid Edge of Earth.* Photographs from Roberta's expedition to Libya in 2002 were also shown in an exhibit, called *Ancient Ruins and Desert Dunes*, at Hoopers Gallery, a posh art gallery in London, England.

This trip to Libya exemplifies Roberta's bravery. When she was there in 2003, the war

with Iraq was just beginning, and things were tense and dangerous. Some tourists had been kidnapped in the area right before she arrived. Roberta had six bodyguards armed with machine guns to escort her through the richly colored Libyan sands.

She also endured a sandstorm. With her tent securely fastened to the side of her SUV, she sealed everything shut and waited. The sand got through the tent's seams and the scarf she wrapped around her head and stabbed at her skin "like millions of needles." In the midst of this, Roberta attempted to videotape the storm!

Recently, Roberta took on another Canadian project, the Burgess Shale fossil bed in British Columbia. Declared a World Heritage Site by the United Nations in 1981, the Burgess Shale represents a unique snapshot of the evolution of life. It contains many otherwise unknown soft-bodied sea creatures that lived 505 million years ago. Roberta explains her motivation for the project:

"A lot of people—especially Canadians—seem to think Canada isn't important to the world...I've been trying to create these big images of the country for people to see otherwise."

Roberta's photographs have been shown in exhibits in the Diane Farris Gallery in Vancouver, British Columbia. In 2009 her latest exhibit, entitled *Canadian Canopies*, featured stunning images of Canada's trees in the colors of the four seasons. Previous exhibits at the Diane Farris Gallery include *Earthland* (2004), photographs of Canada and the far North, and *Deserts in Time* (2006), with work from Roberta's desert expeditions.

There are numerous Bondar photographs for sale from the Diane Farris Gallery, and many of these can be viewed on the Internet. There is quite a variety to choose from, with close-ups of Arctic flowers, majestic mountains, brilliant deserts, and even a view of the Great Lakes from the *Discovery* shuttle! All of them highlight Roberta's distinct style characterized by a love of color, especially blue, and a sense of the patterns and shapes found in nature.

Roberta's photographs are definitely art, but they are art with a purpose. Here is one way that Roberta explains how she wants her photographs to affect people and their response to our planet:

BONDAR'S BOOKS

Bondar, Barbara, and Roberta Bondar. On the Shuttle: Eight Days in Space. *Toronto: Greey de Pencier Books, 1993.*

Bondar, Roberta. Touching the Earth. *Toronto: Key Porter Books, 1994.*

Bondar, Roberta. Passionate Vision: Discovering Canada's National Parks. *Vancouver: Douglas & McIntyre, 2000.*

Bondar, Roberta. Canada: Landscape of Dreams. *Vancouver: Douglas & McIntyre, 2002.*

Bondar, Roberta. The Arid Edge of Earth. *Toronto: Roberta Bondar Astronaut Enterprise, 2006.*

"Very few people have ever
stepped back from the planet
and observed it. Passing over
Canada, I was struck not only
by the country's size, but also by
the incredible amount of water
we have. It's a resource we
need to take the lead in
protecting. And it's easier to want
to protect something if you
have learned to love it."

Roberta loves this planet, her planet, our planet. She wants us all to see its beauty as she sees it—and to feel the same need to protect it.

A Well-Rounded Person

There is more to Roberta Bondar than science and art. In addition to photography, neurology research, and maintaining her practice as a physician, she has many other interests. She's had her private pilot's license since she was 22. She's also licensed as a scuba diver and a parachutist. Her official NASA biography lists among her hobbies biking, hot air ballooning, inline skating, and flying.

Roberta never stops learning. In fact, this is one message she delivers to young people in her talks: Never stop learning. It is a philosophy that Roberta lives. In recent years, she took up golf and within three years became good enough to shoot a respectable 100. With such an adventurous spirit, Roberta is likely to continue to pursue new hobbies and develop new talents for many years to come.

BONDAR'S CAMERAS

As shown below, Roberta Bondar does not use a digital camera to take her spectacular photographs. In a recent interview she stated that she uses a Linhof plate camera. Plate cameras do not use a memory card or even a roll of film. They use a plate of film, just as old-fashioned cameras did before rolls of film were invented. Roberta's photos are taken with large film. Instead of the typical 35mm film (named because it is 35 mm (3.5 cm) wide), Roberta uses cameras that take film that is up to 4 inches (102 mm) wide. Photographs taken on film this big have a very high resolution. When they are blown up large, the details are still crisp and clear.

Chapter 6
For the Love of Earth

Roberta Bondar is the kind of person who follows her dreams. She sets goals, and then she strives with all her might to achieve them. She has not been afraid of change. The activities she has chosen to pursue have all been things that give her pleasure. At the same time, however, Roberta has spent her time with activities that have a positive impact on the world around her.

Influencing Others

From spruce budworm research to medicine to space flight, Roberta's passions have consistently been about things that can make a difference. In 1993, with her time as an astronaut behind her, Roberta began to make other, concrete

She continues to spend much of her time influencing others to join her in her quest to make the world a better place.

contributions to helping her favorite planet. In 1993, she became the leader of the charitable foundation Friends of the Environment, which gives money to local projects across Canada to help people preserve natural environments. She continues to spend much of her time influencing others to join her in her quest to make the world a better place.

Thanks to pioneers like Roberta Bondar—male and female alike—Canadians will be among those who live and work in space for years to come.

Roberta has vigorously pursued many means of educating others around her, including photography and writing. Public speaking has been, and continues to be, a major part of her life. Not only does Roberta speak with elementary, high school, and university students on a regular basis, she also makes appearances to meet with others involved in science clubs, Girl Guides of Canada, and other youth and women's organizations. She speaks to the general public through television and radio programs and is interviewed for newspapers and magazines regularly.

Roberta also speaks to science conferences, governments, and businesses. She is hired

Student reporters at the Roberta Bondar Public School in Ottawa, Ontario, interview Roberta. This school is one of several in Canada that are named after Roberta. Many students want to know more about what Earth looked like from space. Such questions give Roberta the perfect opportunity to pursue one of her passions—convincing others to join in her quest to help our planet.

around the world by companies and organizations such as the pharmaceutical company Pfizer and the FBI to train people in a variety of areas, including creativity, decision making, the environment, values, inventiveness, leadership, and teamwork. As Canada's Honorary Patron for the International Year of Planet Earth 2008, Roberta has helped to raise awareness of the importance of research and education in the field of earth sciences.

When it comes to making lasting changes in society, education is important. Roberta has been active in this area as well. She was chosen to lead a special committee set up by the Ontario Ministry of Education to advise on how best to include teaching about the environment in schools. The report, *Shaping Our Schools, Shaping Our Future*, was published in 2007. It made 32 recommendations, such as supporting school boards to hire staff with the responsibility of overseeing environmental education, developing courses in the environmental sciences, including teaching about the environment in all subject areas—not just science and geography—and setting good examples by being environmentally responsible when building schools and purchasing materials. The Ontario government is following all of the recommendations made by Roberta's committee.

Honored Far and Wide

Roberta's accomplishments have not gone unnoticed. Canada Post issued a stamp in 2003 with her name and photograph on it. It was one of the first stamps in Canada to honor a person who is still living. *Time* magazine named her

DOES ROBERTA BONDAR ALWAYS SUCCEED?

Like most people, Roberta has had her share of setbacks and hard choices. As a teenager, for example, she loved sports and wanted to become a physical education teacher. A case of the mumps left her weak in one side, however, and her chosen career looked unlikely. Roberta pursued science instead. After going up in space with Mission STS–42, Roberta would have liked to have the opportunity to train to be a mission specialist with NASA. She was not considered a good candidate, and this was one reason why Roberta quit her job as an astronaut. One of the secrets to Roberta's success is that when obstacles are put in her way, she simply changes course and finds another goal to strive toward instead.

WATER: WHAT'S THE ISSUE?

Roberta speaks and writes about many environmental challenges. One of them is water. From her vantage point aboard the shuttle, Roberta was struck by the amount of fresh water covering her home country of Canada. She points out in her book *Touching the Earth* that the need for fresh water is more than 35 times greater now than it was 300 years ago. Many cities do not have enough, and many countries cannot meet daily needs. Supplies of fresh water are running out. Water needs to be conserved, sources protected, and new technologies developed to ensure safe water supplies for generations to come.

one of North America's best explorers in the same year. Roberta has also been inducted into the Canadian Medical Hall of Fame and the International Women's Hall of Fame. She has received several medals in admiration of her work, including the Order of Canada for her outstanding contribution to Canadian society. NASA awards to every astronaut who flies into space a Space Flight Medal that features an image of a space shuttle orbiter within a triangular design, so she has one of these, too.

Many universities have celebrated Roberta by giving her an honorary Ph.D. degree. This means of recognizing someone's contributions to society started in the 1400s. Roberta has been honored this way by 24 different universities (and counting) from Alberta to Newfoundland. In addition, Trent University in Peterborough, Ontario, appointed Roberta as their chancellor in 2003.

In this post, Roberta was the ceremonial head of the university, with the job of giving the degrees to graduates and representing the university at events. Roberta was selected for a

beings on the
e have a very
conception of
e need to think
the survival of
t as a whole.
ll we think the
es on forever.
e in space, you
it doesn't."

ndar describes
nvironment is
in Touching
Earth

second three-year term, which was completed in 2009.

One of the biggest honors bestowed on Roberta Bondar has been the naming of several places after her, in recognition of her leadership and commitment to education. To date, there are five schools with "Roberta Bondar" in their names, in British Columbia and Ontario. There are Roberta Bondar scholarships offered by institutions such as the Girl Guides of Canada. Trent University also has a Roberta Bondar scholarship that pays for a scientist who is doing research in Northern and Polar Studies to come to Trent for one year.

Also named after Roberta is a park in her hometown of Sault Ste. Marie, and a flower—the Roberta Bondar rose.

Roberta's Legacy

The success of the missions with Canadians Marc Garneau (1983) and Roberta Bondar (1992) encouraged NASA and the Canadian government to continue their partnership. In 1992, Canadians were once again invited to apply for the job of astronaut. An ad placed in Canadian newspapers by the Canadian Space Agency promising "exciting career opportunities" drew responses from 5,330 applicants. Four people were chosen as the next generation of astronauts.

Following in the footsteps of women like Roberta Bondar and Sally Ride, engineer and pilot Julie Payette was selected. She has since flown in two shuttle missions, the latest in 2009. In 2008, two more Canadian astronauts were chosen out of 5,351 fresh applicants.

Thanks to pioneers like Roberta Bondar—male and female alike—Canadians will be among those who live and work in space for years to come.

On Earth, Roberta also intends to make a lasting impact. She has recently created a foundation in her name that is "dedicated to providing a creative, learner-friendly approach to understanding environmental science." The Roberta Bondar Foundation is a charity that raises money to develop programs that "educate and improve knowledge of the environment." In a 2010 radio interview, Roberta explains:

"I'm very much interested in what I might be able to do in the future in terms of education. So I've started a foundation in my name that is going to be using science and art to get people interested and excited about science and the environment."

Roberta's future is sure to be bursting with arts and science and a burning passion for Earth, and our future will be brighter because of it. Roberta continues to show us what is possible if we try. It is possible for humanity to reach beyond our planet. It is also possible for us, as individuals, to reach beyond ourselves and have a positive impact on the world around us.

The Roberta Bondar rose is a pretty yellow color. It can be seen growing at the Botanical Gardens in Montreal, or you can buy it from a nursery to plant in your own garden.

"Society needs heroes to rejuvenate, re-energize, and renew itself with visions of the possible. That's what heroes do."

Roberta Bondar

Chronology

1945 Roberta Bondar is born on December 2 in Sault Ste. Marie, Ontario, Canada.

1953 Eight-year-old Roberta sends away for a toy space helmet. The U.S. government is experimenting with sending insects and other animals into orbit in small capsules to see what happens to them.

1958 President Dwight D. Eisenhower creates the National Aeronautics and Space Administration, or NASA.

1961 Soviet cosmonaut Yuri Gagarin becomes the first human being to orbit Earth in a spacecraft.

1963 Soviet cosmonaut Valentina Tereshkova orbits Earth on a solo flight for three days to become the first woman in space.

1968 Roberta graduates from the University of Guelph with a Bachelor of Science degree

1969 NASA astronaut Neil Armstrong becomes the first person to walk on the Moon, with the famous words, "... one small step for man, one giant leap for mankind."

1977 Roberta becomes a practicing doctor, with a specialty in neurology—the study of the nervous system.

1983 Canada is invited by NASA to participate in the space shuttle program and send astronauts into space. Canada advertises for astronauts in the newspaper, and Roberta is one of six hired. Sally Ride, a NASA astronaut, is the first American woman in space.

1984 Marc Garneau is the first Canadian to go into space, on Mission 41-G. Roberta is there to greet him when he lands.

1986 The space shuttle *Challenger* explodes shortly after liftoff. All the crew is killed, and NASA's space shuttle program is put on hold indefinitely.

1989 The space shuttle program begins again.

1990 Roberta is selected to join NASA Mission STS–42 and go into space.

1992 On January 22, Roberta flies into space aboard the space shuttle *Discovery*. This makes her the first neurologist in space, the second Canadian in space, and the first Canadian woman in space. For eight days she circles Earth in orbit and returns to ground again on January 30. In April, she is honored as an Officer in the Order of Canada. In September, Roberta quits her job as an astronaut.

1993 Roberta becomes the Chair of the Friends of the Environment Foundation. She also trains in professional nature photography. She writes the children's book *On the Shuttle: Eight Days in Space*, with her sister, Barbara.

1994 Roberta's book *Touching the Earth* is published.

1997 The public views Roberta's photographs for the first time, in a National Gallery of Canada exhibit, *Beauty of Another Order— Photography in Science*.

1998–2000 Roberta photographs all 41 of Canada's National Parks. They are published in a book, *Passionate Vision: Discovering Canada's National Parks*, and the photos tour in an art exhibit.

2003 Canada Post issues the Roberta Bondar astronaut stamp.

Time magazine names her one of North America's best explorers.

2003–2009 Roberta is the Chancellor of Trent University.

2006 Roberta publishes her fourth book, *The Arid Edge of Earth*, which features photographs of the world's deserts and an environmental message.

2007 Roberta leads a Working Group on Environmental Education for the Ontario Ministry of Education. All 32 of the committee's recommendations are being implemented.

2008–2010 Roberta is named Canada's Honorary Patron by the United Nations for the International Year of Planet Earth.

2009 The Roberta Bondar Foundation is begun to further the goal of educating the public and school children about the environment by combining art and science. The fifth public school named after Roberta Bondar opens in Vaughan, Ontario. Four other public schools already bear her name.

2010 The space shuttle is scheduled to be retired and is no longer to be the spacecraft used by NASA.

Glossary

accelerate To increase in speed; to move faster

arteries The tubes that carry blood from the heart throughout the body

atmosphere The layer of gases that surrounds a planet

boreal Referring to the region that makes up about 60 percent of Canada's area. It is characterized by a wide variety of trees and other species of plant and animal wildlife.

cockpit The area in a plane, boat, or spacecraft from where the vehicle is steered or driven

friction The force that resists motion between things in contact. Friction causes moving objects to slow down.

genetics The hereditary makeup of life that governs all aspects of an organism's characteristics

gravity The physical force one object exerts on another through attraction; the bigger the object, the greater the force. The closer an object is to another, the greater the force. Earth's gravity keeps the Moon in its orbit.

ground control The staff members on the ground who monitor and aid the progress of craft in flight

hormone A chemical produced by cells in one part of the body that is released into the body and has an effect on cells in another part of the body

International Microgravity Laboratory (IML) A research laboratory built with the cooperation of many countries to study the effects of microgravity in space

legacy What someone leaves behind; a gift or contribution to society

Mach A number that indicates how fast an object is moving in relation to the speed of sound. Mach 1 is the speed of sound. Mach 2 is twice the speed of sound.

microgravity The conditions in Earth's orbit, where there is very little gravity. There is still a small amount of gravitational force, so microgravity is a more accurate description than "zero gravity."

mission A group of people sent elsewhere to perform a task

molecule The smallest particle of a substance that has all the properties of that substance

module An independent unit that is part of a larger space vehicle

orbit The circular path taken by an object as it travels around another object

Parkinson's disease A disease that usually occurs later in life and is characterized by slow movement, shaking muscles, and difficulty with balance. It is caused by a decrease in the production of the chemical dopamine in the brain.

orbiter The part of the space shuttle that looks like a plane, where the astronauts and payload are housed. It is the only part that orbits Earth.

protein Small molecules that make up the building blocks of life

quarantine A period of isolation to prevent the spread of disease

radiation Energy that is emitted in waves. The Sun's radiation has many wavelengths, such as visible light (sunlight), harmful ultraviolet waves, and microwaves.

rocket An engine that is forced upward by the burning of gas or liquid fuel in a chamber at the bottom of a tube

resolution The measure of the sharpness of an image, which is dependent on the number of tiny points of color in a given area. The more dots of color in an area, the sharper the image will be.

satellite Any object that revolves around Earth; the Moon is a natural satellite. The word satellite is often used to refer specifically to artificial objects that are put into orbit on purpose.

simulate To create an imitation that mimics reality

space shuttle A reusable spacecraft designed to transport people and materials back and forth between Earth and space.

sphere A solid with all points on the surface at an equal distance from its center. A perfect ball has the shape of a sphere.

technology The practical application of knowledge

turbulence Irregular movement or agitation, especially referring to up-and-down motion encountered while moving through air or water

ultrasound A method of viewing what is happening inside the body by using wavelengths that cannot be detected by the human ear. These wavelengths are transmitted into the body and bounce off structures inside, forming a picture that reveals their shape.

wavelength The distance between the adjacent peaks of a wave

weight Relative heaviness; the force with which an object is attracted to Earth. Weight is dependent on both the force of gravity and the mass (amount) of the object.

zoology The study of animal life

Further Information

Books

Bondar, Barbara, and Roberta Bondar. *On the Shuttle: Eight Days in Space.* Toronto: Greey de Pencier Books, 1993.

Bondar, Roberta. *Touching the Earth.*
Toronto: Key Porter Books, 1994.

Bondar, Roberta. *Passionate Vision: Discovering Canada's National Parks.* Vancouver: Douglas & McIntyre, 2000.

Bondar, Roberta. *Canada: Landscape of Dreams.*
Vancouver: Douglas & McIntyre, 2002.

Bondar, Roberta. *The Arid Edge of Earth.*
Toronto: Roberta Bondar Astronaut Enterprise, 2006.

Dotto, Lydia. *The Astronauts: Canada's Voyageurs in Space.*
Stoddard Publishing, 1993.

Gueldenpfennig, Sonia. *Spectacular Women in Space.*
Second Story Press, 2004.

Web sites

www.robertabondar.com
Choose which Roberta Bondar you'd like to learn about: the author, photographer, scientist, astronaut, business consultant, or media spokesperson. Explore some of the topics Bondar speaks to the public about and read an official biography.

www.therobertabondarfoundation.org
Learn more about Roberta Bondar's latest initiative—to combine the arts and sciences to encourage education about the environment.

www.dianefarrisgallery.com/artist/bondar/
The Diane Farris Gallery exhibits Roberta Bondar's photographs and handles their sale. In addition to having many of Roberta's fabulous photographs online, this website has some excellent biographical information about Roberta, as well as links to some articles written about her in recent years.

www.jsc.nasa.gov/Bios/PS/bondar.html
NASA's official biography of Roberta Bondar is a good way to compare her background and achievements with other astronauts, past and present.

http://archives.cbc.ca/science_technology/space/clips/2633/
Watch and listen to Canadian Broadcasting Corporation (CBC) coverage of Roberta Bondar's launch into space. See her wave and shout to the media on her way to the launch pad.

www.asc-csa.gc.ca/eng/default.asp
The website for the Canadian Space Agency features write-ups on all Canada's astronauts, past and present, as well as details of Canada's contributions to space, including the Canadarm and Canadarm2. Videos, interviews, details of space missions, statistics, news, and the science of space are readily available here.

http://spaceflight.nasa.gov/home/index.html
Search the NASA database of photographs taken from space, view statistics of every shuttle mission, and track real-time data, including live TV coverage of the International Space Station—24/7.

Video

Destiny in Space, IMAX Corporation, 1994.

Index

Index

About the Author

Judy Wearing is the author of **Edison's Concrete Piano**, a book about failure and success, as well as many children's books in science and history, some of them for Crabtree Publishing. Like Roberta Bondar, she grew up in Northern Ontario, took zoology and agriculture courses at the University of Guelph, and attended the University of Western Ontario. She lives on a hobby farm in eastern Ontario, surrounded by animals.